ABOUT THIS PUBLICATION

FOR SERVICE ASSISTANCE

Customer Service Department
704.898.0770

www.visionbooks.org

TID: 4989020
ISBN (10) digit: 1502302209
ISBN (13) digit: 978-1502302205

123-4-56789-01237-Paperback
123-4-56789-01237-Hardback

First Edition

090520140547

Printed in the United States of America

North Carolina Criminal Law

And Procedure-Pamphlet # 4

Printed In conjunction with the Administration of the Courts

North Carolina Criminal Law and Procedure
Pamphlet Reference Guide

10

11

12

13

14

§ 7A-171.2. Qualifications for nomination or renomination.

(a)   In order to be eligible for nomination or for renomination as a magistrate an individual shall be a resident of the county for which he is appointed.

(b)   To be eligible for nomination as a magistrate, an individual shall have at least eight years' experience as the clerk of superior court in a county of this State or shall have a four-year degree from an accredited senior institution of higher education or shall have a two-year associate degree and four years of work experience in a related field, including teaching, social services, law enforcement, arbitration or mediation, the court system, or counseling. The Administrative Officer of the Courts may determine whether the work experience is sufficiently related to the duties of the office of magistrate for the purposes of this subsection. In determining whether an individual's work experience is in a related field, the Administrative Officer of the Courts shall consider the requisite knowledge, skills, and abilities for the office of magistrate.

The eligibility requirements prescribed by this subsection do not apply to individuals holding the office of magistrate on June 30, 1994, and do not apply to individuals who have been nominated by June 30, 1994, but who have not been appointed or taken the oath of office by that date.

(c)   In order to be eligible for renomination as a magistrate an individual shall have successfully completed the course of basic training for magistrates prescribed by G.S. 7A-177.

(d)   Notwithstanding any other provision of this subsection, an individual who holds the office of magistrate on July 1, 1977, shall not be required to have successfully completed the course of basic training for magistrates prescribed by G.S. 7A-177 in order to be eligible for renomination as a magistrate. (1977, c. 945, s. 6; 1993 (Reg. Sess., 1994), c. 769, s. 7.13(a); 2003-381, s. 1.)

§ 7A-172. Repealed by Session Laws 1977, c. 945, s. 5.

§ 7A-173. Suspension; removal; reinstatement.

(a)   A magistrate may be suspended from performing the duties of his office by the chief district judge of the district court district in which his county is located, or removed from office by the senior regular resident superior court judge of, or any regular superior court judge holding court in, the district or set of districts as defined in G.S. 7A-41.1(a) in which the county is located. Grounds for suspension or removal are the same as for a judge of the General Court of Justice.

(b) Suspension from performing the duties of the office may be ordered upon filing of sworn written charges in the office of clerk of superior court for the county in which the magistrate resides. If the chief district judge, upon examination of the sworn charges, finds that the charges, if true, constitute grounds for removal, he may enter an order suspending the magistrate from performing the duties of his office until a final determination of the charges on the merits. During suspension the salary of the magistrate continues.

(c) If a hearing, with or without suspension, is ordered, the magistrate against whom the charges have been made shall be given immediate written notice of the proceedings and a true copy of the charges, and the matter shall be set by the chief district judge for hearing before the senior regular resident superior court judge or a regular superior court judge holding court in the district or set of districts as defined in G.S. 7A-41.1(a) in which the county is located. The hearing shall be held in a county within the district or set of districts not less than 10 days nor more than 30 days after the magistrate has received a copy of the charges. The hearing shall be open to the public. All testimony offered shall be recorded. At the hearing the superior court judge shall receive evidence, and make findings of fact and conclusions of law. If he finds that grounds for removal exist, he shall enter an order permanently removing the magistrate from office, and terminating his salary. If he finds that no such grounds exist, he shall terminate the suspension, if any.

(d) A magistrate may appeal from an order of removal to the Court of Appeals on the basis of error of law by the superior court judge. Pending decision of the case on appeal, the magistrate shall not perform any of the duties of his office. If, upon final determination, he is ordered reinstated, either by the appellate division or by the superior court on remand, his salary shall be restored from the date of the original order of removal. (1965, c. 310, s. 1; 1967, c. 108, s. 4; 1973, c. 148, ss. 3, 4; 1987 (Reg. Sess., 1988), c. 1037, s. 18.)

§ 7A-174. Bonds.

Prior to taking office, magistrates shall be bonded, individually or collectively, in such amount or amounts as the Administrative Officer of the Courts shall determine. The bond or bonds shall be conditioned upon the faithful performance of the duties of the office of magistrate. The Administrative Officer shall procure such bond or bonds from any indemnity or guaranty company authorized to do business in North Carolina, and the premium or premiums shall be paid by the State. (1965, c. 310, s. 1.)

§ 7A-175. Records to be kept.

A magistrate shall keep such dockets, accounts, and other records, under the general supervision of the clerk of superior court, as may be prescribed by the Administrative Office of the Courts. (1965, c. 310, s. 1.)

§ 7A-176. Office of justice of the peace abolished.

The office of justice of the peace is abolished in each county upon the establishment of a district court therein. (1965, c. 310, s. 1.)

§ 7A-177. Training course in duties of magistrate.

(a)   Within six months of taking the oath of office as a magistrate for the first time, a magistrate is required to attend and satisfactorily complete a course of basic training of at least 40 hours in the civil and criminal duties of a magistrate. The Administrative Office of the Courts is authorized to contract with the School of Government at the University of North Carolina at Chapel Hill or with any other qualified educational organization to conduct this training, and to reimburse magistrates for travel and subsistence expenses incurred in taking such training.

(b)   In addition to the basic training course required under subsection (a) of this section, continuing education courses shall be provided at such times and locations as necessary to assure that they are conveniently available to all magistrates without extensive travel to other parts of the State. (1975, c. 956, s. 11; 1983 (Reg. Sess., 1984), c. 1116, s. 87; 2006-264, s. 29(a); 2007-393, s. 15; 2007-484, s. 25.5; 2008-187, s. 2.)

§ 7A-178. Magistrate as child support hearing officer.

A magistrate who meets the qualifications of G.S. 50-39 and is properly designated pursuant to G.S. Chapter 50, Article 2, to serve as a child support hearing officer, may serve in that capacity and has the authority and responsibility assigned to child support hearing officers by Chapter 50. (1985 (Reg. Sess., 1986), c. 993, s. 2.)

§ 7A-179. Reserved for future codification purposes.

Article 17.

Clerical Functions in the District Court.

§ 7A-180. Functions of clerk of superior court in district court matters.

The clerk of superior court:

(1)   Has and exercises all of the judicial powers and duties in respect of actions and proceedings pending from time to time in the district court of his county which are now or hereafter conferred or imposed upon him by law in respect of actions and proceedings pending in the superior court of his county;

(2)   Performs all of the clerical, administrative and fiscal functions required in the operation of the district court of his county in the same manner as he is required to perform such functions in the operation of the superior court of his county;

(3)   Maintains, under the supervision of the Administrative Office of the Courts, an office of uniform consolidated records of all judicial proceedings in the superior court division and the district court division of the General Court of Justice in his county. Those records shall include civil actions, special proceedings, estates, criminal actions, juvenile actions, minutes of the court and all other records required by law to be maintained. The form and procedure for filing, docketing, indexing, and recording shall be as prescribed by the Administrative Officer of the Courts notwithstanding any contrary statutory provision as to the title and form of the record or as a method of indexing;

(4)   Has the power to accept written appearances, waivers of trial or hearing and pleas of guilty or admissions of responsibility for the types of offenses specified in G.S. 7A-273(2) in accordance with the schedules of offenses

18

promulgated by the Conference of Chief District Judges pursuant to G.S. 7A-148, and in such cases, to enter judgment and collect the fine or penalty and costs;

(5)   Has the power to issue warrants of arrest valid throughout the State, and search warrants valid throughout the county of the issuing clerk;

(6)   Has the power to conduct an initial appearance in accordance with Chapter 15A, Article 24, Initial Appearance, and to fix conditions of release in accordance with Chapter 15A, Article 26, Bail;

(7)   Continues to exercise all powers, duties and authority theretofore vested in or imposed upon clerks of superior court by general law, with the exception of jurisdiction in juvenile matters; and

(8)   Has the power to accept written appearances, waivers of trial and pleas of guilty to violations of G.S. 14-107 when restitution, including service charges and processing fees allowed under G.S. 14-107, is made, the amount of the check is two thousand dollars ($2,000) or less, and the warrant does not charge a fourth or subsequent violation of this statute, and, in such cases, to enter such judgments as the chief district judge shall direct and, forward the amounts collected as restitution to the appropriate prosecuting witnesses and to collect the costs.

(9)   Repealed by Session Laws 1991 (Reg. Sess., 1992), c. 900, s. 118(c). (1965, c. 310, s. 1; 1967, c. 691, s. 16; 1969, c. 1190, s. 14; 1973, c. 503, ss. 3, 4; c. 1286, s. 6; 1975, c. 166, s. 23; c. 626, s. 2; 1981, c. 142; 1983, c. 586, s. 4; 1985, c. 425, s. 3, c. 764, s. 10; 1985 (Reg. Sess., 1986), c. 852, s. 17; 1987, c. 355, s. 3; 1989 (Reg. Sess., 1990), c. 1041, s. 2; 1991, c. 520, s. 1; 1991 (Reg. Sess., 1992), c. 900, s. 118(c); 1993, c. 374, s. 3.)

§ 7A-181. Functions of assistant and deputy clerks of superior court in district court matters.

Assistant and deputy clerks of superior court:

(1)   Have the same powers and duties with respect to matters in the district court division as they have in the superior court division;

(2)   Have the same powers as the clerk of superior court with respect to the issuance of warrants and acceptance of written appearances, waivers of trial and pleas of guilty; and

(3)   Have the same power as the clerk of superior court to fix conditions of release in accordance with Chapter 15A, Article 26, Bail, and the same power as the clerk of superior court to conduct an initial appearance in accordance with Chapter 15A, Article 24, Initial Appearance. (1965, c. 310, s. 1; 1967, c. 691, s. 17; 1973, c. 503, s. 5; 1975, c. 166, s. 24; c. 626, s. 3.)

§ 7A-182. Clerical functions at additional seats of court.

(a)   In any county in which the General Assembly has authorized the district court to hold sessions at a place or places in addition to the county seat, the clerk of superior court shall furnish assistant and deputy clerks to the extent necessary to process efficiently the judicial business at such additional seat or seats of court. Only such records as are necessary for the expeditious processing of current judicial business shall be kept at the additional seat or seats of court. The office of the clerk of superior court at the county seat shall remain the permanent depository of official records.

(b)   If an additional seat of a district court is designated for any municipality located in more than one county of a district, the clerical functions for that seat of court shall be provided by the clerks of superior court of the contiguous counties, in accordance with standing rules issued by the chief district judge, after consultation with the clerks concerned and a committee of the district bar appointed for this purpose. An assistant or deputy clerk assigned to a seat of district court described in this subsection shall have the same powers and authority as if he were acting in his own county. (1965, c. 310, s. 1; 1967, c. 691, s. 18; 1969, c. 1190, s. 15.)

§ 7A-183. Clerk or assistant clerk as child support hearing officer.

A clerk or assistant clerk of superior court who meets the qualifications of G.S. 50-39 and is properly designated pursuant to G.S. Chapter 50, Article 2, to serve as a child support hearing officer, may serve in that capacity and has the authority and responsibility assigned to child support hearing officers by Chapter 50. (1985 (Reg. Sess., 1986), c. 993, s. 3.)

20

§§ 7A-184 through 7A-189. Reserved for future codification purposes.

Article 18.

District Court Practice and Procedure Generally.

§ 7A-190. District courts always open.

The district courts shall be deemed always open for the disposition of matters properly cognizable by them. But all trials on the merits shall be conducted at trial sessions regularly scheduled as provided in this Chapter. (1965, c. 310, s. 1.)

§ 7A-191. Trials; hearings and orders in chambers.

All trials on the merits and all hearings on infractions conducted pursuant to Article 66 of Chapter 15A shall be conducted in open court and so far as convenient in a regular courtroom. All other proceedings, hearings, and acts may be done or conducted by a judge in chambers in the absence of the clerk or other court officials and at any place within the district; but no hearing may be held, nor order entered, in any cause outside the district in which it is pending without the consent of all parties affected thereby. (1965, c. 310, s. 1; 1985, c. 764, s. 11; 1985 (Reg. Sess., 1986), c. 852, s. 17.)

§ 7A-191.1. Recording of proceeding in which defendant pleads guilty or no contest to felony in district court.

The trial judge shall require that a true, complete, and accurate record be made of the proceeding in which a defendant pleads guilty or no contest to a Class H or I felony pursuant to G.S. 7A-272. (1995 (Reg. Sess., 1996), c. 725, s. 4.)

§ 7A-192. By whom power of district court to enter interlocutory orders exercised.

Any district judge may hear motions and enter interlocutory orders in causes regularly calendared for trial or for the disposition of motions, at any session to which the district judge has been assigned to preside. The chief district judge

21

and any district judge designated by written order or rule of the chief district judge, may in chambers hear motions and enter interlocutory orders in all causes pending in the district courts of the district, including causes transferred from the superior court to the district court under the provisions of this Chapter. The designation is effective from the time filed in the office of the clerk of superior court of each county of the district until revoked or amended by written order of the chief district judge. (1965, c. 310, s. 1; 1969, c. 1190, s. 16.)

§ 7A-193. Civil procedure generally.

Except as otherwise provided in this Chapter, the civil procedure provided in Chapters 1 and 1A of the General Statutes applies in the district court division of the General Court of Justice. Where there is reference in Chapters 1 and 1A of the General Statutes to the superior court, it shall be deemed to refer also to the district court in respect of causes in the district court division. (1965, c. 310, s. 1; 1969, c. 1190, s. 17.)

§ 7A-194. Repealed by Session Laws 1977, c. 711, s. 33.

§ 7A-195. Repealed by Session Laws 1969, c. 911, s. 5.

§ 7A-196. Jury trials.

(a)   In civil cases in the district court there shall be a right to trial by a jury of 12 in conformity with Rules 38 and 39 of the Rules of Civil Procedure.

(b)   In criminal cases there shall be no jury trials in the district court. Upon appeal to superior court trial shall be de novo, with jury trial as provided by law.

(c)   In adjudicatory hearings for infractions, there shall be no right to trial by jury in the district court. (1965, c. 310, s. 1; 1967, c. 954, s. 3; 1985, c. 764, s. 12; 1985 (Reg. Sess., 1986), c. 852, s. 17.)

§ 7A-197. Petit jurors.

Unless otherwise provided in this Chapter, the provisions of Chapter 9 of the General Statutes with respect to petit jurors for the trial of civil actions in the

superior court are applicable to the trial of civil actions in the district court.
(1965, c. 310, s. 1.)

§ 7A-198. Reporting of civil trials.

(a)   Court-reporting personnel shall be utilized, if available, for the reporting of civil trials in the district court. If court reporters are not available in any county, electronic or other mechanical devices shall be provided by the Administrative Office of the Courts upon request of the chief district judge.

(b)   The Administrative Office of the Courts shall from time to time investigate the state of the art and techniques of recording testimony, and shall provide such electronic or mechanical devices as are found to be most efficient for this purpose.

(c)   If an electronic or other mechanical device is utilized, it shall be the duty of the clerk of the superior court or some other person designated by him to operate the device while a trial is in progress, and the clerk shall thereafter preserve the record thus produced, which may be transcribed, as required, by any person designated by the Administrative Office of the Courts. If stenotype, shorthand, or stenomask equipment is used, the original tapes, notes, discs, or other records are the property of the State, and the clerk shall keep them in his custody.

(d)   Reporting of any trial may be waived by consent of the parties.

(e)   Reporting will not be provided in trials before magistrates or in hearings to adjudicate and dispose of infractions in the district court.

(f)   Appointment of a reporter or reporters for district court proceedings in each district court district shall be made by the chief district judge for that district. The compensation and allowances of reporters in each district shall be fixed by the chief district judge, within limits determined by the Administrative Officer of the Courts, and paid by the State.

(g)   A party to a civil trial in district court may request a private agreement from the opposing party or parties to share equally in the cost of a court reporter to be selected from a list provided by the Administrative Office of the Courts. If the opposing party does not consent to share this cost, the requesting party may nevertheless pay to have a court reporter present to record the trial and, in the event that the opposing party appeals the case, that party shall reimburse the party providing the court reporter in full for the costs incurred for the court reporter's services and transcripts.

In the event that the recording device in a civil trial conducted without a court reporter fails for any reason to provide a reasonably accurate record of the trial for purposes of appeal, then the trial judge shall grant a motion for a new trial made by a losing party whose request pursuant to this section to share the cost of a court reporter was not consented to by the opposing party. (1965, c. 310, s. 1; 1969, c. 1190, s. 18; 1985, c. 764, s. 13; 1985 (Reg. Sess., 1986), c. 852, s. 17; 1987, c. 384, s. 2; 1987 (Reg. Sess., 1988), c. 1037, s. 19; 1996, 2nd Ex. Sess., c. 18, s. 22.11.)

§ 7A-199. Special venue rule when district court sits without jury in seat of court lying in more than one county; where judgments recorded.

(a)   In any nonjury civil action or juvenile matter properly pending in the district court division, regularly assigned for a hearing or trial before a district judge at a seat of the district court in a municipality the corporate limits of which extend into two or more contiguous counties, venue is properly laid for such trial or hearing if by statute or common law it is properly laid in any of the contiguous counties.

(b)   In any jury civil action regularly assigned for a hearing or trial before a district judge at a seat of the district court in a municipality the corporate limits of which extend into two or more contiguous counties, venue is properly laid for such jury trial if by statute or common law it is properly laid in any of the contiguous counties; provided, however, any such action shall be instituted in the county of proper venue, and the jurors summoned shall be from the county where such action was instituted. Notwithstanding the fact that the place of trial within such municipality is in a different county from the county where such action was commenced, the sheriff of the county where such action was commenced is authorized to summon the jurors to appear at such place of trial. Such jurors shall be subject to the same challenge as other jurors, except challenges for nonresidence in the county of trial.

(c)   A district court judge sitting at a seat of court described in this section may, in criminal cases, conduct preliminary hearings and try misdemeanors arising within the corporate limits of the municipality plus the territory embraced within a distance of one mile in all directions therefrom.

If the corporate limits of the municipality extend into two or more counties, each of which is in a separate district court district, a district court judge assigned to sit at the seat of court has the same authority over criminal cases arising in the municipality and the territory embraced within a distance of one mile in all directions that he would have if the corporate limits of the municipality were solely located in a single district court district. Judges assigned to sit in such a municipality shall be assigned by the chief district court judge serving the district in which a majority of the voters of the municipality reside, but offenses arising in a portion of the municipality in which a minority of the voters reside shall not be disposed of in the municipality unless the chief district court judge for that district consents in writing to the disposition of criminal cases in the municipality. However, for charges brought by municipal law enforcement officers only, if the corporate limits of the municipality extend into four or more counties, each of which is in a separate district court district, offenses arising in a portion of the municipality in which a minority of the voters reside shall be disposed of in the portion of the municipality in which a majority of the voters reside without obtaining the consent of the chief district court judge for the district in which the offense occurred.

(d)   The judgment or order rendered in any civil action or juvenile matter heard or tried under the authority of this section shall be recorded in the county where the action was commenced. The judgment or finding of probable cause or other determination in any criminal action heard or tried under the authority of this section shall be recorded in the county where the offense was committed. (1967, c. 691, s. 19; 1989, c. 795, s. 23(c2); 2009-398, s. 1.)

§ 7A-200. District and set of districts defined; chief district court judges and their authority.

(a)   In this section:

(1)   "District" means any district court district established by G.S. 7A-133 which consists exclusively of one or more entire counties;

(2)   "Set of districts" means any set of two or more district court districts established under G.S. 7A-133, none of which consists exclusively of one or more entire counties, but both or all of which include territory from the same county or counties and together comprise all of the territory of that county or those counties; "set of districts" also means a set of three district court districts

25

in one county, one consisting of the entire county and the other two consisting of parts of that county; and

(3)   "Chief district court judge" means in the case of a set of districts, the chief district court judge for those districts, designated by the chief justice from among the district court judges for the districts in the set of districts.

(b)   Whenever by law a duty is imposed upon the chief district court judge, it means for a set of districts the chief district court judge designated under subsection (a)(3) of this section. (1995, c. 507, s. 21.1(a); 2007-484, s. 25(c).)

§§ 7A-201 through 7A-209. Reserved for future codification purposes.

Article 19.

Small Claim Actions in District Court.

§ 7A-210. Small claim action defined.

For purposes of this Article a small claim action is a civil action wherein:

(1)   The amount in controversy, computed in accordance with G.S. 7A-243, does not exceed ten thousand dollars ($10,000); and

(2)   The only principal relief prayed is monetary, or the recovery of specific personal property, or summary ejectment, or any combination of the foregoing in properly joined claims; and

(3)   The plaintiff has requested assignment to a magistrate in the manner provided in this Article.

The seeking of the ancillary remedy of claim and delivery or an order from the clerk of superior court for the relinquishment of property subject to a lien pursuant to G.S 44A-4(a) does not prevent an action otherwise qualifying as a small claim under this Article from so qualifying. (1965, c. 310, s. 1; 1973, c. 1267, s. 1; 1979, c. 144, s. 1; 1981, c. 555, s. 1; 1985, c. 329; c. 655, s. 1; 1989, c. 311, s. 1; 1993, c. 107, s. 1; c. 553, s. 73(a); 1999-411, s. 1; 2004-128, s. 1; 2013-159, s. 1.)

26

§ 7A-211. Small claim actions assignable to magistrates.

In the interest of speedy and convenient determination, the chief district judge may, in his discretion, by specific order or general rule, assign to any magistrate of his district any small claim action pending in his district if the defendant is a resident of the county in which the magistrate resides. If there is more than one defendant, at least one of them must be a bona fide resident of the county in which the magistrate resides. (1965, c. 310, s. 1, 1967, c. 1165.)

§ 7A-211.1. Actions to enforce motor vehicle mechanic and storage liens.

Notwithstanding the provisions of G.S. 7A-210(2) and 7A-211, the chief district judge may in his discretion, by specific order or general rule, assign to any magistrate of his district actions to enforce motor vehicle mechanic and storage liens arising under G.S. 44A-2(d) or 20-77(d) when the claim arose in the county in which the magistrate resides. The defendant may be subjected to the jurisdiction of the court over his person by the methods provided in G.S. 7A-217 or 1A-1, Rules 4(j) and 4(j1), Rules of Civil Procedure. (1977, c. 86, s. 1; 1979, c. 602, s. 1; 2000-185, s. 1.)

§ 7A-212. Judgment of magistrate in civil action improperly assigned or not assigned.

No judgment of the district court rendered by a magistrate in a civil action assigned to him by the chief district judge is void, voidable, or irregular for the reason that the action is not one properly assignable to the magistrate under this article. The sole remedy for improper assignment is appeal for trial de novo before a district judge in the manner provided in this article. No judgment rendered by a magistrate in a civil action is valid when the action was not assigned to him by the chief district judge. (1965, c. 310, s. 1.)

§ 7A-213. Procedure for commencement of action; request for and notice of assignment.

The plaintiff files his complaint in a small claim action in the office of the clerk of superior court of the county wherein the defendant, or one of the defendants resides. The designation "Small Claim" on the face of the complaint is a request for assignment. If, pursuant to order or rule, the action is assigned to a

27

magistrate, the clerk issues a magistrate summons substantially in the form prescribed in this Article as soon as practicable after the assignment is made. The issuance of a magistrate summons commences the action. After service of the magistrate summons on the defendant, the clerk gives written notice of the assignment to the plaintiff. The notice of assignment identifies the action, designates the magistrate to whom assignment is made, and specifies the time, date and place of trial. By any convenient means the clerk notifies the magistrate of the assignment and the setting. (1965, c. 310, s. 1; 1969, c. 1190, s. 19; 1971, c. 377, s. 9.)

§ 7A-214. Time within which trial is set.

The time for trial of a small claim action is set not later than 30 days after the action is commenced. Except in an action demanding summary ejectment, if the time set for trial is earlier than five days after service of the magistrate summons, the magistrate shall order a continuance. By consent of all parties the time for trial may be changed from the time set. For good cause shown, the magistrate to whom the action is assigned may grant continuances from time to time. (1965, c. 310, s. 1; 2009-359, s. 1.)

§ 7A-215. Procedure upon nonassignment of small claim action.

Failure of the chief district judge to assign a claim within five days after filing of a complaint requesting its assignment constitutes nonassignment. The chief district judge may sooner order nonassignment. Upon nonassignment, the clerk immediately issues summons in the manner and form provided for commencement of civil actions generally, whereupon process is served, return made, and pleadings are required to be filed in the manner provided for civil actions generally. Upon issuing civil summons, the clerk gives written notice of nonassignment to the plaintiff. The plaintiff within five days after notice of nonassignment, and the defendant before or with the filing of his answer, may request a jury trial. Failure within the times so limited to request a jury trial constitutes a waiver of the right thereto. Upon the joining of issue, the clerk places the action upon the civil issue docket for trial in the district court division. (1965, c. 310, s. 1.)

§ 7A-216. Form of complaint.

28

The complaint in a small claim action shall be in writing, signed by the party or his attorney, except the complaint in an action for summary ejectment may be signed by an agent for the plaintiff. It need be in no particular form, but is sufficient if in a form which enables a person of common understanding to know what is meant. In any event, the forms prescribed in this Article are sufficient under this requirement, and are intended to indicate the simplicity and brevity of statement contemplated. Demurrers and motions to challenge the legal and formal sufficiency of a complaint in an assigned small claim action shall not be used. But at any time after its filing, the clerk, the chief district judge, or the magistrate to whom such an action is assigned may, on oral or written ex parte motion of the defendant, or on his own motion, order the plaintiff to perfect the statement of his claim before proceeding to its determination, and shall grant extensions of time to plead and continuances of trial pending any perfecting of statement ordered. (1965, c. 310, s. 1; 1971, c. 377, s. 10.)

§ 7A-217. Methods of subjecting person of defendant to jurisdiction.

When by order or rule a small claim action is assigned to a magistrate, the court may obtain jurisdiction over the person of the defendant by the following methods:

(1)   By delivering a copy of the summons and of the complaint to the defendant or by leaving copies thereof at the defendant's dwelling house or usual place of abode with some person of suitable age and discretion then residing therein. When the defendant is under any legal disability, the defendant may be subjected to personal jurisdiction only by personal service of process in the manner provided by G.S. 1A-1, Rule 4(j)(2).

(2)   When the defendant is not under any legal disability, the defendant may be served by registered or certified mail, signature confirmation, or designated delivery service as provided in G.S. 1A-1, Rule 4(j). Proof of service is as provided in G.S. 1A-1, Rule 4(j2).

(3)   When the defendant is under no legal disability, the defendant may be subjected to the jurisdiction of the court over the person of the defendant by written acceptance of service or by voluntary appearance.

(4)   In summary ejectment cases only, service as provided in G.S. 42-29 is also authorized. (1965, c. 310, s. 1; 1969, c. 1190, s. 20; 1973, c. 90; 1983, c. 332, s. 3; 2011-332, s. 1.1.)

§ 7A-218. Answer of defendant.

At any time prior to the time set for trial, the defendant may file a written answer admitting or denying all or any of the allegations in the complaint, or pleading new matter in avoidance. No particular form is required, but it is sufficient if in a form to enable a person of common understanding to know the nature of the defense intended. A general denial of all the allegations of the complaint is permissible.

Failure of defendant to file a written answer after being subjected to the jurisdiction of the court over his person constitutes a general denial. (1965, c. 310, s. 1; 1967, c. 691, s. 20.)

§ 7A-219. Certain counterclaims; cross claims; third-party claims not permissible.

No counterclaim, cross claim or third-party claim which would make the amount in controversy exceed the jurisdictional amount established by G.S. 7A-210(1) is permissible in a small claim action assigned to a magistrate. No determination of fact or law in an assigned small claim action estops a party thereto in any subsequent action which, except for this section, might have been asserted under the Code of Civil Procedure as a counterclaim in the small claim action. Notwithstanding G.S. 1A-1, Rule 13, failure by a defendant to file a counterclaim in a small claims action assigned to a magistrate, or failure by a defendant to appeal a judgment in a small claims action to district court, shall not bar such claims in a separate action. (1965, c. 310, s. 1; 1973, c. 1267, s. 2; 1979, c. 144, s. 2; 1981, c. 555, s. 2; 1985, c. 329; 1989, c. 311, s. 2; 1993, c. 553, s. 73(b); 2005-423, s. 9.)

§ 7A-220. No required pleadings other than complaint.

There are no required pleadings in assigned small claim actions other than the complaint. Answers and counterclaims may be filed by the defendant in accordance with G.S. 7A-218 and G.S. 7A-219. Any new matter pleaded in avoidance in the answer is deemed denied or avoided. On appeal from the judgment of the magistrate for trial de novo before a district judge, the judge shall allow appropriate counterclaims, cross claims, third party claims, replies, and answers to cross claims, in accordance with G.S. 1A-1, et seq. (1965, c. 310, s. 1; 1987, c. 628.)

§ 7A-221. Objections to venue and jurisdiction over person.

By motion prior to filing answer, or in the answer, the defendant may object that the venue is improper, or move for change of venue, or object to the jurisdiction of the court over his person. These motions or objections are heard on notice by the chief district judge or a district judge designated by order or rule of the chief district judge. Assignment to the magistrate is suspended pending determination of the objection, and the clerk gives notice of the suspension by any convenient means to the magistrate to whom the action has been assigned. All these objections are waived if not made prior to the date set for trial. If venue is determined to be improper, or is ordered changed, the action is transferred to the district court of the new venue, and is not thereafter assigned to a magistrate, but proceeds as in the case of civil actions generally. (1965, c. 310, s. 1.)

§ 7A-222. General trial practice and procedure.

(a)   Trial of a small claim action before a magistrate is without a jury. The rules of evidence applicable in the trial of civil actions generally are observed. At the conclusion of plaintiff's evidence the magistrate may render judgment of dismissal if plaintiff has failed to establish a prima facie case. If a judgment of dismissal is not rendered the defendant may introduce evidence. At the conclusion of all the evidence the magistrate may render judgment or may in his discretion reserve judgment for a period not in excess of 10 days, except as provided in subsection (b) of this section.

(b)   In a small claim action for summary ejectment, the magistrate shall render judgment on the same day on which the conclusion of all the evidence and submission of legal authorities occurs, unless the parties concur on an extension of additional time for entering the judgment and except for more complex summary ejectment cases, in which event the magistrate shall render judgment within five business days of the hearing. Complex summary ejectment cases include cases brought for criminal activity, breaches other than nonpayment of rent, evictions involving SECTION 8 of the Housing Act of 1937 (42 U.S.C. § 1437f) or public housing tenants, and cases with counterclaims. (1965, c. 310, s. 1; 1971, c. 377, s. 11; 2013-334, s. 1.)

§ 7A-223. Practice and procedure in small claim actions for summary ejectment.

(a)   In any small claim action demanding summary ejectment or past due rent, or both, the complaint may be signed by an agent acting for the plaintiff who has actual knowledge of the facts alleged in the complaint. If a small claim action demanding summary ejectment is assigned to a magistrate, the practice and procedure prescribed for commencement, form and service of process, assignment, pleadings, and trial in small claim actions generally are observed, except that if the defendant by written answer denies the title of the plaintiff, the action is placed on the civil issue docket of the district court division for trial before a district judge. In such event, the clerk withdraws assignment of the action from the magistrate and immediately gives written notice of withdrawal, by any convenient means, to the plaintiff and the magistrate to whom the action has been assigned. The plaintiff, within five days after receipt of the notice, and the defendant, in his answer, may request trial by jury. Failure to request jury trial within the time limited is a waiver of the right to trial by jury.

(b)   If either party in a small claim action for summary ejectment moves for a continuance, the magistrate shall render a decision on the motion in accordance with Rule 40(b) of the Rules of Civil Procedure. The magistrate shall not continue a matter for more than five days or until the next session of small claims court, whichever is longer, without the consent of both parties.

(c)   The Administrative Office of the Courts is directed to develop a form for parties in small claim actions for summary ejectment to inform them of the time line and process in summary ejectment actions. The clerk of superior court shall make the form available to the parties. (1965, c. 310, s. 1; 1967, c. 691, s. 21; 1971, c. 377, s. 12; 2013-334, ss. 2, 6.)

§ 7A-224. Rendition and entry of judgment.

Judgment in a small claim action is rendered in writing and signed by the magistrate. The judgment so rendered is a judgment of the district court, and is recorded and indexed as are judgments of the district and superior court generally. Entry is made as soon as practicable after rendition. (1965, c. 310, s. 1; 1969, c. 1190, s. 21.)

§ 7A-225. Lien and execution of judgment.

From the time of docketing, the judgment rendered by a magistrate in a small claim action constitutes a lien and is subject to execution in the manner provided in Chapter 1, Article 28, of the General Statutes. (1965, c. 310, s. 1.)

§ 7A-226. Priority of judgment when appeal taken.

When appeal is taken from a judgment in a small claim action, the lien acquired by docketing merges into any judgment rendered after trial de novo on appeal, continues as a lien from the first docketing, and has priority over any judgment docketed subsequent to the first docketing. (1965, c. 310, s. 1.)

§ 7A-227. Stay of execution on appeal.

Appeal from judgment of a magistrate does not stay execution if the judgment is for recovery of specific property. Such execution may be stayed by order of the clerk of superior court upon petition by the appellant accompanied by undertaking in writing, executed by one or more sufficient sureties approved by the clerk, to the effect that if judgment be rendered against appellant the sureties will pay the amount thereof with costs awarded against the appellant. Appeal from judgment of a magistrate does stay execution if the judgment is for money damages. This section shall not require any undertaking of appellants in summary ejectment actions other than those imposed by Chapter 42 of the General Statutes. (1965, c. 310, s. 1; 1967, c. 24, s. 1; 1977, c. 844; 1979, c. 820, s. 9.)

§ 7A-228. New trial before magistrate; appeal for trial de novo; how appeal perfected; oral notice; dismissal.

(a)   The chief district court judge may authorize magistrates to hear motions to set aside an order or judgment pursuant to G.S. 1A-1, Rule 60(b)(1) and order a new trial before a magistrate. The exercise of the authority of the chief district court judge in allowing magistrates to hear Rule 60(b)(1) motions shall not be construed to limit the authority of the district court to hear motions pursuant to Rule 60(b)(1) through (6) of the Rules of Civil Procedure for relief from a judgment or order entered by a magistrate and, if granted, to order a new trial before a magistrate. After final disposition before the magistrate, the sole remedy for an aggrieved party is appeal for trial de novo before a district court judge or a jury. Notice of appeal may be given orally in open court upon announcement or after entry of judgment. If not announced in open court, written notice of appeal must be filed in the office of the clerk of superior court within 10 days after entry of judgment. The appeal must be perfected in the manner set out in subsection (b). Upon announcement of the appeal in open court or upon receipt of the written notice of appeal, the appeal shall be noted upon the judgment. If the judgment was mailed to the parties, then the time computations for appeal of such judgment shall be pursuant to G.S. 1A-1, Rule 6.

(b)   The appeal shall be perfected by (1) oral announcement of appeal in open court; or (2) by filing notice of appeal in the office of the clerk of superior court within 10 days after entry of judgment pursuant to subsection (a), and by serving a copy of the notice of appeal on all parties pursuant to G.S. 1A-1, Rule 5. Failure to pay the costs of court to appeal within 10 days after entry of judgment in a summary ejectment action, and within 20 days after entry of judgment in all other actions, shall result in the automatic dismissal of the appeal. Notwithstanding the foregoing deadlines, if an appealing party petitions to qualify as an indigent for the appeal and is denied, that party shall have an additional five days to perfect the appeal by paying the court costs. The failure to demand a trial by jury in district court by the appealing party before the time to perfect the appeal has expired is a waiver of the right thereto.

(b1)   A person desiring to appeal as an indigent shall, within 10 days of entry of judgment by the magistrate, file an affidavit that he or she is unable by reason of poverty to pay the costs of appeal. Within 20 days after entry of judgment, a superior or district court judge, magistrate, or the clerk of the superior court may authorize a person to appeal to district court as an indigent if the person is unable to pay the costs of appeal. The clerk of superior court shall authorize a person to appeal as an indigent if the person files the required affidavit and meets one or more of the criteria listed in G.S. 1-110. A superior or district court judge, a magistrate, or the clerk of the superior court may authorize a person who does not meet any of the criteria listed in G.S. 1-110 to appeal as an indigent if the person cannot pay the costs of appeal.

The district court may dismiss an appeal and require the person filing the appeal to pay the court costs advanced if the allegations contained in the affidavit are determined to be untrue or if the court is satisfied that the action is frivolous or malicious. If the court dismisses the appeal, the court shall affirm the judgment of the magistrate.

34

(c)   Whenever such appeal is docketed and is regularly set for trial, and the appellant fails to appear and prosecute his appeal, the presiding judge may have the appellant called and the appeal dismissed; and in such case the judgment of the magistrate shall be affirmed.

(d)   When a defendant in a summary ejectment action has given notice of appeal and perfected the appeal in accordance with G.S. 7A-228(b), the plaintiff may serve upon the defendant a motion to dismiss the appeal if the defendant:

(1)   Failed to raise a defense orally or in writing in the small claims court;

(2)   Failed to file a motion, answer, or counterclaim in the district court; and

(3)   Failed to make any payment due under any applicable bond to stay execution of the judgment for possession.

The motion to dismiss the appeal shall list all of the deficiencies committed by the defendant, as described in subdivisions (1), (2), and (3) of this subsection, and shall state that the court will decide the motion to dismiss without a hearing if the defendant fails to respond within 10 days of receipt of the motion. The defendant may defeat the motion to dismiss by responding within 10 days of receipt of the motion by doing any of the following acts: (i) filing a responsive motion, answer, or counterclaim and serving the plaintiff with a copy thereof or (ii) paying the amount due under the bond to stay execution. The court shall review the file, determine whether the motion satisfies the requirements of this subsection, determine whether the defendant has made a sufficient response to defeat the motion, and shall enter an order resolving the matter without a hearing. (1965, c. 310, s. 1; 1969, c. 1190, s. 22; 1979, 2nd Sess., c. 1328, s. 3; 1981, c. 599, s. 3; 1985, c. 753, ss. 1, 2; 1987, c. 553; 1993, c. 435, s. 2; 1998-120, s. 1; 2013-334, s. 3.)

§ 7A-229. Trial de novo on appeal.

Upon appeal noted, the clerk of superior court places the action upon the civil issue docket of the district court division. The district judge before whom the action is tried may order repleading or further pleading by some or all of the parties; may try the action on stipulation as to the issue; or may try it on the pleadings as filed. (1965, c. 310, s. 1.)

§ 7A-230. Jury trial on appeal.

The appellant in his written notice of appeal may demand a jury on the trial de novo. Within 10 days after receipt of the notice of appeal stating that the costs of the appeal have been paid, any appellee by written notice served on all parties and on the clerk of superior court may demand a jury on the trial de novo. (1965, c. 310, s. 1; 1981, c. 599, s. 3.)

§ 7A-231. Provisional and incidental remedies.

The provisional and incidental remedies of claim and delivery, subpoena duces tecum, production of documents and orders for the relinquishment of property subject to a possessory lien pursuant to G.S. 44A-4(a) are obtainable in small claims actions. The practice and procedure provided therefor in respect of civil actions generally is observed, conformed as may be required. No other provisional or incidental remedies are obtainable while the action is pending before the magistrate. (1965, c. 310, s. 1; 1985, c. 655, s. 3.)

§ 7A-232. Forms.

The following forms are sufficient for the purposes indicated under this article. Substantial conformity is sufficient.

FORM 1.

MAGISTRATE SUMMONS

NORTH CAROLINA   General Court of Justice

District Court Division

_____COUNTY   Before the Magistrate

A. B., Plaintiff

v.   SUMMONS

C. D., Defendant

To the above-named Defendant:

You are hereby summoned to appear before His Honor_____, Magistrate of the District Court, at _____ (time)_____, on ____ (date)____, at the _____ (address) _____in the _____ (city)_____, then and there to defend against proof of the claim stated in the complaint filed in this action, copy of which is served herewith. You may file written answer making defense to the claim in the office of the Clerk of Superior Court _____ County in_____, N. C., not later than the time set for trial. If you do not file answer, plaintiff must nevertheless prove his claim before the Magistrate. But if you fail to appear and defend against the proof offered, judgment for the relief demanded in the complaint may be rendered against you.

This _____ day of _____ (month)_____, _____.

_____

Clerk of Superior Court

_____County

FORM 2.

NOTICE OF NON-ASSIGNMENT OF ACTION

NORTH CAROLINA   General Court of Justice

District Court Division

_____County

A. B., Plaintiff

v.   NOTICE OF NON-ASSIGNMENT

C. D., Defendant   OF ACTION

To the above-named Plaintiff:

Take notice that the civil action styled as above which you requested be assigned for trial before a Magistrate will not be assigned. Thirty-day summons to answer is being issued for service upon defendant, and upon the joining of issue this action will be placed on the civil issue docket for trial before a district judge.

This _____ day of _____ (month)_____, _____.

Clerk of Superior Court

_____County

FORM 3.

39

NOTICE OF ASSIGNMENT OF ACTION

NORTH CAROLINA   General Court of Justice

District Court Division

_____COUNTY   Before the Magistrate

A. B., Plaintiff

v.   NOTICE OF ASSIGNMENT

C. D., Defendant   OF ACTION

To the above-named Plaintiff:

Take notice that the civil action styled as above, commenced by you as plaintiff, has been assigned for trial before His Honor_____, Magistrate of the District Court, at _____ (time) _____on_____ (date)_____, at _____ (address) _____in _____ (city)_____, N.C.

_____
  Clerk of Superior Court

_____County

FORM 4.

COMPLAINT ON A PROMISSORY NOTE

NORTH CAROLINA   General Court of Justice

District Court Division

_____COUNTY   SMALL CLAIM

A. B., Plaintiff

v.   COMPLAINT

C. D., Defendant

1. Plaintiff is a resident of _____ County; defendant is a resident of _____ County.

2. Defendant on or about January 1, 1964, executed and delivered to plaintiff a promissory note (in the following words and figures: (here set out the note verbatim)); (a copy of which is annexed as Exhibit_____); (whereby defendant promised to pay to plaintiff or order on June 1, 1964, the sum of two hundred and fifty dollars ($250.00) with interest thereon at the rate of six percent (6%) per annum).

3. Defendant owes the plaintiff the amount of said note and interest.

Wherefore plaintiff demands judgment against defendant for the sum of two hundred and fifty dollars ($250.00), interest and costs.

This _____ day of_____, _____

_____

(signed) A. B., Plaintiff

(or E. F., Attorney for Plaintiff)

Service by mail is, is not, requested.

_____

(signed) A. B., Plaintiff

(or E. F., Attorney for Plaintiff)

FORM 5.

COMPLAINT ON AN ACCOUNT

(Caption as in form 4)

1. (Allegation of residence of parties)

2. Defendant owes plaintiff two hundred and fifty dollars ($250.00) according to the account annexed as Exhibit A.

Wherefore (etc., as in form 4).

43

FORM 6.

COMPLAINT FOR GOODS SOLD AND DELIVERED

(Caption as in form 4)

1. (Allegation of residence of parties)

2. Defendant owes plaintiff two hundred and fifty dollars ($250.00) for goods sold and delivered to defendant between June 1, 1965, and December 1, 1965.

Wherefore (etc., as in form 4).

FORM 7.

COMPLAINT FOR MONEY LENT

(Caption as in form 4)

1. (Allegation of residence of parties)

2. Defendant owes plaintiff two hundred and fifty dollars ($250.00) for money lent by plaintiff to defendant on or about June 1, 1965.

Wherefore (etc., as in form 4.)

FORM 8.

COMPLAINT FOR CONVERSION

(Caption as in form 4)

1. (Allegation of residence of parties)

2. On or about June 1, 1965, defendant converted to his own use a set of plumbing tools of the value of two hundred and fifty dollars ($250.00), the property of plaintiff.

Wherefore (etc., as in form 4).

FORM 9.

COMPLAINT FOR INJURY TO PERSON OR PROPERTY

(Caption as in form 4)

1. (Allegation of residence of parties)

2. On or about June 1, 1965, at the intersection of Main and Church Streets in the Town of Ashley, N. C., defendant (intentionally struck plaintiff a blow in the face) (negligently drove a bicycle into plaintiff) (intentionally tore plaintiff's clothing) (negligently drove a motorcycle into the side of plaintiff's automobile).

3. As a result (plaintiff suffered great pain of body and mind, and incurred expenses for medical attention and hospitalization in the sum of one hundred and fifty dollars ($150.00) (plaintiff suffered damage to his property above described in the sum of two hundred and fifty dollars ($250.00).

Wherefore (etc., as in form 4).

FORM 10.

COMPLAINT TO RECOVER POSSESSION OF CHATTEL

(Caption as in form 4)

1. (Allegation of residence of parties)

2. Defendant has in his possession a set of plumber's tools of the value of two hundred dollars ($200.00), the property of plaintiff. Plaintiff is entitled to immediate possession of the same but defendant refuses on demand to deliver the same to plaintiff.

46

3. Defendant has unlawfully kept possession of the property above described since on or about June 1, 1965, and has thereby deprived plaintiff of its use, to his damage in the sum of fifty dollars ($50.00).

Wherefore plaintiff demands judgment against defendant for the recovery of possession of the property above described and for the sum of fifty dollars ($50.00), interest and costs. (etc., as in form 4).

FORM 11.

COMPLAINT IN SUMMARY EJECTMENT

(Caption as in form 4)

1. (Allegation of residence of parties)

2. Defendant entered into possession of a tract of land (briefly described) as a lessee of plaintiff (or as lessee of E. F. who, after making the lease, assigned his estate to the plaintiff); the term of defendant expired on the 1st day of June, 1965 (or his term has ceased by nonpayment of rent, or otherwise, as the fact may be); the plaintiff has demanded possession of the premises of the defendant, who refused to surrender it, but holds over; the estate of plaintiff is still subsisting, and the plaintiff is entitled to immediate possession.

3. Defendant owes plaintiff the sum of fifty dollars ($50.00) for rent of the premises from the 1st of May, 1965, to the 1st day of June, 1965, and one hundred dollars ($100.00) for the occupation of the premises since the 1st day of June, 1965 to the present.

Wherefore, plaintiff demands judgment against defendant that he be put in immediate possession of the premises, and that he recover the sum of one hundred and fifty dollars ($150.00), interest and costs. (etc., as in form 4). (1965, c. 310, s. 1; 1971, c. 1181, s. 2; 1999-456, s. 59.)

§§ 7A-233 through 7A-239. Reserved for future codification purposes.
SUBCHAPTER V. JURISDICTION AND POWERS OF THE TRIAL DIVISIONS OF THE GENERAL COURT OF JUSTICE.

Article 20.

Original Civil Jurisdiction of the Trial Divisions.

§ 7A-240. Original civil jurisdiction generally.

Except for the original jurisdiction in respect of claims against the State which is vested in the Supreme Court, original general jurisdiction of all justiciable matters of a civil nature cognizable in the General Court of Justice is vested in the aggregate in the superior court division and the district court division as the trial divisions of the General Court of Justice. Except in respect of proceedings in probate and the administration of decedents' estates, the original civil jurisdiction so vested in the trial divisions is vested concurrently in each division. (1965, c. 310, s. 1.)

§ 7A-241. Original jurisdiction in probate and administration of decedents' estates.

Exclusive original jurisdiction for the probate of wills and the administration of decedents' estates is vested in the superior court division, and is exercised by the superior courts and by the clerks of superior court as ex officio judges of probate according to the practice and procedure provided by law. (1965, c. 310, s. 1.)

§ 7A-242. Concurrently held original jurisdiction allocated between trial divisions.

For the efficient administration of justice in respect of civil matters as to which the trial divisions have concurrent original jurisdiction, the respective divisions are constituted proper or improper for the trial and determination of specific actions and proceedings in accordance with the allocations provided in this Article. But no judgment rendered by any court of the trial divisions in any civil action or proceeding as to which the trial divisions have concurrent original jurisdiction is void or voidable for the sole reason that it was rendered by the court of a trial division which by such allocation is improper for the trial and determination of the civil action or proceeding. (1965, c. 310, s. 1.)

§ 7A-243. Proper division for trial of civil actions generally determined by amount in controversy.

Except as otherwise provided in this Article, the district court division is the proper division for the trial of all civil actions in which the amount in controversy is twenty-five thousand dollars ($25,000) or less; and the superior court division is the proper division for the trial of all civil actions in which the amount in controversy exceeds twenty-five thousand dollars ($25,000).

For purposes of determining the amount in controversy, the following rules apply whether the relief prayed is monetary or nonmonetary, or both, and with respect to claims asserted by complaint, counterclaim, cross-complaint or third-party complaint:

(1)   The amount in controversy is computed without regard to interest and costs.

(2)   Where monetary relief is prayed, the amount prayed for is in controversy unless the pleading in question shows to a legal certainty that the amount claimed cannot be recovered under the applicable measure of damages. The value of any property seized in attachment, claim and delivery, or other ancillary proceeding, is not in controversy and is not considered in determining the amount in controversy.

(3)   Where no monetary relief is sought, but the relief sought would establish, enforce, or avoid an obligation, right or title, the value of the obligation, right, or title is in controversy. Where the owner or legal possessor of property seeks recovery of property on which a lien is asserted pursuant to G.S. 44A-4(a) the amount in controversy is that portion of the asserted lien which is disputed. The judge may require by rule or order that parties make a good faith estimate of the value of any nonmonetary relief sought.

(4)   a.   Except as provided in subparagraph c of this subdivision, where a single party asserts two or more properly joined claims, the claims are aggregated in computing the amount in controversy.

b.   Except as provided in subparagraph c, where there are two or more parties properly joined in an action and their interests are aligned, their claims are aggregated in computing the amount in controversy.

49

c.   No claims are aggregated which are mutually exclusive and in the alternative, or which are successive, in the sense that satisfaction of one claim will bar recovery upon the other.

d.   Where there are two or more claims not subject to aggregation the highest claim is the amount in controversy.

(5)   Where the value of the relief to a claimant differs from the cost thereof to an opposing party, the higher amount is used in determining the amount in controversy. (1965, c. 310, s. 1; 1981 (Reg. Sess., 1982), c. 1225; 1985, c. 655, s. 2; 2013-159, s. 2.)

§ 7A-244. Domestic relations.

The district court division is the proper division without regard to the amount in controversy, for the trial of civil actions and proceedings for annulment, divorce, equitable distribution of property, alimony, child support, child custody and the enforcement of separation or property settlement agreements between spouses, or recovery for the breach thereof. (1965, c. 310, s. 1; 1981, c. 815, s. 5; 1987, c. 573, s. 1.)

§ 7A-245. Injunctive and declaratory relief to enforce or invalidate statutes; constitutional rights.

(a)   The superior court division is the proper division without regard to the amount in controversy, for the trial of civil actions where the principal relief prayed is

(1)   Injunctive relief against the enforcement of any statute, ordinance, or regulation;

(2)   Injunctive relief to compel enforcement of any statute, ordinance, or regulation;

(3)   Declaratory relief to establish or disestablish the validity of any statute, ordinance, or regulation; or

(4)   The enforcement or declaration of any claim of constitutional right.

50

(b)   When a case is otherwise properly in the district court division, a prayer for injunctive or declaratory relief by any party not a plaintiff on grounds stated in this section is not ground for transfer. (1965, c. 310, s. 1.)

§ 7A-246. Special proceedings; exceptions; guardianship and trust administration.

The superior court division is the proper division, without regard to the amount in controversy, for the hearing and trial of all special proceedings except proceedings under the Protection of the Abused, Neglected or Exploited Disabled Adult Act (Chapter 108A, Article 6, of the General Statutes), proceedings for involuntary commitment to treatment facilities (Chapter 122C, Article 5, of the General Statutes), adoption proceedings (Chapter 48 of the General Statutes) and of all proceedings involving the appointment of guardians and the administration by legal guardians and trustees of express trusts of the estates of their wards and beneficiaries, according to the practice and procedure provided by law for the particular proceeding. (1965, c. 310, s. 1; 1973, c. 726, s. 5; c. 1378, s. 3; 1981, c. 682, s. 1; 1985, c. 689, s. 4; 1995, c. 88, s. 7.)

§ 7A-247. Quo warranto.

The superior court division is the proper division, without regard to the amount in controversy, for the trial of all civil actions seeking as principal relief the remedy of quo warranto, according to the practice and procedure provided for obtaining that remedy. (1965, c. 310, s. 1; 1971, c. 377, s. 13.)

§ 7A-248. Condemnation actions and proceedings.

The superior court division is the proper division, without regard to the amount in controversy, for the trial of all actions and proceedings wherein property is being taken by condemnation in exercise of the power of eminent domain, according to the practice and procedure provided by law for the particular action or proceeding. Nothing in this section is in derogation of the validity of such administrative or quasi-judicial procedures for value appraisal as may be provided for the particular action or proceeding prior to the raising of justiciable issues of fact or law requiring determination in the superior court. (1965, c. 310, s. 1.)

§ 7A-249. Corporate receiverships.

The superior court division is the proper division, without regard to the amount in controversy, for actions for corporate receiverships under Chapter 1, Article 38, of the General Statutes, and proceedings under Chapters 55 (North Carolina Business Corporation Act) and 55A (Nonprofit Corporation Act) of the General Statutes. (1965, c. 310, s. 1; 1973, c. 503, s. 6; 1989 (Reg. Sess., 1990), c. 1024, s. 3.)

§ 7A-250. Review of decisions of administrative agencies.

(a)   Except as otherwise provided in subsections (b) and (c) of this section, the superior court division is the proper division, without regard to the amount in controversy, for review by original action or proceeding, or by appeal, of the decisions of administrative agencies, according to the practice and procedure provided for the particular action, proceeding, or appeal.

(b)   The Court of Appeals shall have jurisdiction to review final orders or decisions of the North Carolina Utilities Commission and the North Carolina Industrial Commission, as provided in Article 5 of this Chapter, and any order or decision of the Commissioner of Insurance described in G.S. 58-2-80.

(c)   Appeals from rulings of county game commissions shall be heard in the district court division. The appeal shall be heard de novo before a district court judge sitting in the county in which the game commission whose ruling is being appealed is located. (1965, c. 310, s. 1; 1967, c. 108, s. 6; 1973, c. 503, s. 7; 1981, c. 444.)

§ 7A-251. Appeal from clerk to judge.

(a)   In all matters properly cognizable in the superior court division which are heard originally before the clerk of superior court, appeals lie to the judge of superior court having jurisdiction from all orders and judgments of the clerk for review in all matters of law or legal inference, in accordance with the procedure provided in Chapter 1 of the General Statutes.

(b)   In all matters properly cognizable in the district court division which are heard originally before the clerk of superior court, appeals lie to the judge of district court having jurisdiction from all orders and judgments of the clerk for review in all matters of law or legal inference, in accordance with the procedure provided in Chapter 1 of the General Statutes. (1965, c. 310, s. 1; 1995, c. 88, s. 8.)

§ 7A-252. Repealed by Session Laws 1971, c. 377, s. 32.

§ 7A-253. Infractions.

Except as provided in G.S. 7A-271(d), original, exclusive jurisdiction for the adjudication and disposition of infractions lies in the district court division. (1985, c. 764, s. 14; 1985 (Reg. Sess., 1986), c. 852, s. 17.)

§ 7A-254. Reserved for future codification purposes.

Article 21.

Institution, Docketing, and Transferring Civil Causes in the Trial Divisions.

§ 7A-255. Clerk of superior court processes all actions and proceedings.

All civil actions and proceedings in the General Court of Justice are instituted in, and the original records thereof are maintained in, the office of the clerk of superior court, without regard to the trial divisions in which the cause is pending from time to time. When the commencement of an action or proceeding requires issuance of summons, the clerk of superior court issues the summons, and such summons runs and is valid as general process of the State without regard to the trial division in which the action or proceeding may be pending from time to time. (1965, c. 310, s. 1; 1967, c. 691, s. 22.)

§ 7A-256. Causes docketed and retained in originally designated trial division until transferred.

Upon the institution of any action or proceeding in the General Court of Justice the party instituting it designates upon the face of the originating pleading or other originating paper when filed, which trial division of the General Court of

53

Justice he deems proper for disposition of the cause. The clerk dockets the cause for the trial division so designated and the cause is retained for complete disposition in that division unless thereafter transferred in accordance with the provisions of this Article. If no designation is made the clerk dockets the cause for the superior court division, and the cause is retained for complete disposition in that division unless thereafter transferred in accordance with the provisions of this Article. (1965, c. 310, s. 1.)

§ 7A-257. Waiver of proper division.

Any party may move for transfer between the trial divisions as provided in this Article. Failure of a party to move for transfer within the time prescribed is a waiver of any objection to the division, except that there shall be no waiver of the jurisdiction of the superior court division in probate of wills and administration of decedents' estates. Where more than one party is aligned in interest, any party may move for transfer of the entire case, notwithstanding waiver by other parties or coparties. A waiver of objection to the division does not prevent the judge from ordering a transfer on his own motion as provided in this Article. (1965, c. 310, s. 1.)

§ 7A-258. Motion to transfer.

(a)   Any party, including the plaintiff, may move on notice to all parties to transfer the civil action or special proceeding to the proper division when the division in which the case is pending is improper under the rules stated in this Subchapter. A motion to transfer to another division may also be made if all parties to the action or proceeding consent thereto, and if the judge deems the transfer will facilitate the efficient administration of justice.

(b)   A motion to transfer is filed in the action or proceeding sought to be transferred, but it is heard and determined by a judge of the superior court division whether the case is pending in that division or not. A superior court judge who has jurisdiction under G.S. 7A-47.1 or G.S. 7A-48 in the district or set of districts as defined in G.S. 7A-41.1(a) in which the county is located, may hear and determine such motion. The motion is heard and determined in a county within that district or set of districts, except by consent of the parties.

(c)   A motion to transfer by any party other than the plaintiff must be filed within 30 days after the moving party is served with a copy of the pleading which

54

justifies transfer. A motion to transfer by the plaintiff, if based upon the pleading of any other party, must be filed within 20 days after the pleading has been filed. A motion to transfer by any party, based upon an amendment to his own pleading must be made not later than 10 days after such amendment is filed. In no event is a motion to transfer made or determined after the case has been called for trial. Failure to move for transfer within the required time is a waiver of any objection to the division in which the case is pending, except in matters of probate of wills or administration of decedents' estates.

(d)   A motion to transfer is in writing and contains:

(1)   A short and direct statement of the grounds for transfer with specific reference to the provision of this Chapter which determines the proper division; and

(2)   A statement by an attorney for the moving party, or if the party is not represented by counsel, a statement by the party that the motion is made in the good faith belief that it may be properly granted and that he intends no amendment which would affect propriety of transfer.

(e)   A motion to transfer is made on notice to all parties.

(f)   Objection to the jurisdiction of the court over person or property is waived when a motion to transfer is filed unless such objection is raised at the time of filing or before. In no other case does the filing of a motion to transfer waive any rights under other motions or pleadings, nor does it prevent the filing of other motions or pleadings, except as provided in Rule 12 of the Rules of Civil Procedure. The filing of a motion to transfer does not stay further proceedings in the case except that:

(1)   Involuntary dismissal is not ordered while a motion to transfer is pending;

(2)   Assignment to a magistrate is not ordered while a motion to transfer is pending; and

(3)   A change of venue is not ordered while a motion to transfer is pending, except by consent.

When a change of venue is ordered by consent while a motion to transfer is pending, the motion to transfer is determined in the new venue. The filing of a motion to transfer does not enlarge the time for filing responsive pleadings, nor does the filing of any other motion or pleading waive any rights under the motion to transfer.

(g)   The motion for transfer provided herein is the sole method for seeking a transfer, and no transfer is effected by the use of mandamus, injunction, prohibition, certiorari, or other extraordinary writs; provided, however, that transfer may be sought in a responsive pleading when permitted by Rules 7(b) and 12(b) of the Rules of Civil Procedure.

(h)   Transfer is effected when an order of transfer is filed. When transfer is ordered, the clerk makes appropriate entries on the dockets of each division and transfers the file of the case to the new division. No further proceedings are taken in the division from which the case is transferred. Papers filed after a transfer are properly filed notwithstanding any erroneous reference to the division from which the case is transferred. All orders made prior to transfer including restraining orders, remain effective after transfer, as if no transfer had been made, until modified or set aside in the division to which the case is transferred.

(i)   A claim of new or different relief asserted after transfer has been effected does not authorize a second transfer. (1965, c. 310, s. 1; 1967, c. 954, s. 3; 1969, c. 1190, s. 22 1/2; 1971, c. 377, s. 14; 1987 (Reg. Sess., 1988), c. 1037, s. 20.)

§ 7A-259. Transfer on judge's own motion.

(a)   If no party has moved for transfer within the time allowed to parties, any superior court judge who may hear and determine motions to transfer may order a transfer upon his own motion for the purpose of efficient administration of the trial divisions at any time before the case is calendared for trial. Transfer is not made on the judge's own motion unless the pleadings clearly show that the case is pending in an improper division. No hearing is held on such transfers, but the parties are given prompt notice when transfer is effected. Nothing in this section affects the power of the clerk to transfer matters and proceedings pending before him when an issue of fact is raised.

(b)   When a district court is established in a district, any superior court judge authorized to hear and determine motions to transfer may, on his own motion, subject to the requirements of subsection (a), transfer to the district court cases pending in the superior court. (1965, c. 310, s. 1; 1967, c. 691, s. 23.)

§ 7A-260. Review of transfer matters.

Orders transferring or refusing to transfer are not immediately appealable, even for abuse of discretion. Such orders are reviewable only by the appellate division on appeal from a final judgment. If on review, such an order is found erroneous, reversal or remand is not granted unless prejudice is shown. If, on review, a new trial or partial new trial is ordered for other reasons, the appellate division may specify the proper division for new trial and order a transfer thereto. (1965, c. 310, s. 1; 1967, c. 108, s. 7.)

§ 7A-261. Repealed by Session Laws 1971, c. 377, s. 32.

§§ 7A-262 through 7A-269. Reserved for future codification purposes.

Article 22.

Jurisdiction of the Trial Divisions in Criminal Actions.

§ 7A-270. Generally.

General jurisdiction for the trial of criminal actions is vested in the superior court and the district court divisions of the General Court of Justice. (1965, c. 310, s. 1.)

§ 7A-271. Jurisdiction of superior court.

(a)   The superior court has exclusive, original jurisdiction over all criminal actions not assigned to the district court division by this Article, except that the superior court has jurisdiction to try a misdemeanor:
(1)   Which is a lesser included offense of a felony on which an indictment has been returned, or a felony information as to which an indictment has been properly waived; or

(2)   When the charge is initiated by presentment; or

(3)   Which may be properly consolidated for trial with a felony under G.S. 15A-926;

(4)   To which a plea of guilty or nolo contendere is tendered in lieu of a felony charge; or

(5)   When a misdemeanor conviction is appealed to the superior court for trial de novo, to accept a guilty plea to a lesser included or related charge.

(b)   Appeals by the State or the defendant from the district court are to the superior court. The jurisdiction of the superior court over misdemeanors appealed from the district court to the superior court for trial de novo is the same as the district court had in the first instance, and when that conviction resulted from a plea arrangement between the defendant and the State pursuant to which misdemeanor charges were dismissed, reduced, or modified, to try those charges in the form and to the extent that they subsisted in the district court immediately prior to entry of the defendant and the State of the plea arrangement.

(c)   When a district court is established in a district, any superior court judge presiding over a criminal session of court shall order transferred to the district court any pending misdemeanor which does not fall within the provisions of subsection (a), and which is not pending in the superior court on appeal from a lower court.

(d)   The criminal jurisdiction of the superior court includes the jurisdiction to dispose of infractions only in the following circumstances:

(1)   If the infraction is a lesser-included violation of a criminal action properly before the court, the court must submit the infraction for the jury's consideration in factually appropriate cases.

(2)   If the infraction is a lesser-included violation of a criminal action properly before the court, or if it is a related charge, the court may accept admissions of responsibility for the infraction. A proper pleading for the criminal action is sufficient to support a finding of responsibility for the lesser-included infraction.

(e)   The superior court has exclusive jurisdiction over all hearings held pursuant to G.S. 15A-1345(e) where the district court had accepted a defendant's plea of guilty or no contest to a felony under the provisions of G.S.

7A-272(c), except that the district court shall have jurisdiction to hear these matters with the consent of the State and the defendant.

(f)   The superior court has exclusive jurisdiction over all hearings to revoke probation pursuant to G.S. 15A-1345(e) where the district court is supervising a drug treatment court or therapeutic court probation judgment under G.S. 7A-272(e), except that the district court has jurisdiction to conduct the revocation proceedings when the chief district court judge and the senior resident superior court judge agree that it is in the interest of justice that the proceedings be conducted by the district court. If the district court exercises jurisdiction under this subsection to revoke probation, appeal of an order revoking probation is to the appellate division. (1965, c. 310, s. 1; 1967, c. 691, s. 24; 1969, c. 1190, ss. 23, 24; 1971, c. 377, s. 15; 1977, c. 711, s. 6; 1979, 2nd Sess., c. 1328, s. 2; 1985, c. 764, s. 15; 1985 (Reg. Sess., 1986), c. 852, s. 17; 2004-128, s. 2; 2009-452, s. 1; 2009-516, s. 7(a), (b); 2010-96, s. 26(a); 2010-97, s. 13.)

§ 7A-272. Jurisdiction of district court; concurrent jurisdiction in guilty or no contest pleas for certain felony offenses; appellate and appropriate relief procedures applicable.

(a)   Except as provided in this Article, the district court has exclusive, original jurisdiction for the trial of criminal actions, including municipal ordinance violations, below the grade of felony, and the same are hereby declared to be petty misdemeanors.

(b)   The district court has jurisdiction to conduct preliminary examinations and to bind the accused over for trial upon waiver of preliminary examination or upon a finding of probable cause, making appropriate orders as to bail or commitment.

(c)   With the consent of the presiding district court judge, the prosecutor, and the defendant, the district court has jurisdiction to accept a defendant's plea of guilty or no contest to a Class H or I felony if:

(1)   The defendant is charged with a felony in an information filed pursuant to G.S. 15A-644.1, the felony is pending in district court, and the defendant has not been indicted for the offense; or

(2)   The defendant has been indicted for a criminal offense but the defendant's case is transferred from superior court to district court pursuant to G.S. 15A-1029.1.

(d)   Provisions in Chapter 15A of the General Statutes apply to a plea authorized under subsection (c) of this section as if the plea had been entered in superior court, so that a district court judge is authorized to act in these matters in the same manner as a superior court judge would be authorized to act if the plea had been entered in superior court, and appeals that are authorized in these matters are to the appellate division.

(e)   With the consent of the chief district court judge and the senior resident superior court judge, the district court has jurisdiction to preside over the supervision of a probation judgment entered in superior court in which the defendant is required to participate in a drug treatment court program pursuant to G.S. 15A-1343(b1)(2b) or a therapeutic court as defined in subsection (f) of this section, or is participating in the drug treatment court pursuant to a deferred prosecution agreement under G.S. 15A-1341(a2). The district court may modify or extend the probation judgment, but jurisdiction to revoke probation supervised under this subsection is as provided in G.S. 7A-271(f).

(f)   As used in subsection (e) of this section, the term "therapeutic court" refers to a court, other than drug treatment court established pursuant to Article 62 of Chapter 7A of the General Statutes, in which a criminal defendant, either as a condition of probation or pursuant to a deferred prosecution agreement under G.S. 15A-1341, is ordered to participate in specified activities designed to address underlying problems of substance abuse and mental illness that contribute to the person's criminal activity. The ordered activities shall, at a minimum, require the person to participate in treatment and attend regular court sessions of the therapeutic court over an extended period of time. The senior resident superior court judge and the chief district court judge shall agree in writing that the therapeutic court is being established and shall file the written agreement with the Administrative Office of the Courts before jurisdiction established by subsection (e) of this section may be exercised by the district court. (1965, c. 310, s. 1; 1995 (Reg. Sess., 1996), c. 725, ss. 1, 2; 2009-452, s. 2; 2009-516, s. 8(a), (b); 2010-96, s. 26(b); 2010-97, s. 13.)

§ 7A-273. Powers of magistrates in infractions or criminal actions.

In criminal actions or infractions, any magistrate has power:

(1)   In infraction cases in which the maximum penalty that can be imposed is not more than fifty dollars ($50.00), exclusive of costs, or in Class 3 misdemeanors, other than the types of infractions and misdemeanors specified in subdivision (2) of this section, to accept guilty pleas or admissions of responsibility and enter judgment;

(2)   In misdemeanor or infraction cases involving alcohol offenses under Chapter 18B of the General Statutes, traffic offenses, hunting, fishing, State park and recreation area rule offenses under Chapter 113 of the General Statutes, boating offenses under Chapter 75A of the General Statutes, and littering offenses under G.S. 14-399(c) and G.S. 14-399(c1), to accept written appearances, waivers of trial or hearing and pleas of guilty or admissions of responsibility, in accordance with the schedule of offenses and fines or penalties promulgated by the Conference of Chief District Judges pursuant to G.S. 7A-148, and in such cases, to enter judgment and collect the fines or penalties and costs;

(2a)   In misdemeanor cases involving the violation of a county ordinance authorized by law regulating the use of dune or beach buggies or other power-driven vehicles specified by the governing body of the county on the foreshore, beach strand, or the barrier dune system, to accept written appearances, waivers of trial or hearing, and pleas of guilty or admissions of responsibility, in accordance with the schedule of offenses and fines or penalties promulgated by the Conference of Chief District Court Judges pursuant to G.S. 7A-148, and in such cases, to enter judgment and collect the fines or penalties and costs;

(3)   To issue arrest warrants valid throughout the State;

(4)   To issue search warrants valid throughout the county;

(5)   To grant bail before trial for any noncapital offense;

(6)   Notwithstanding the provisions of subdivision (1) of this section, to hear and enter judgment as the chief district judge shall direct in all worthless check cases brought under G.S. 14-107, when the amount of the check is two thousand dollars ($2,000) or less. Provided, however, that under this section magistrates may not impose a prison sentence longer than 30 days;

(7)   To conduct an initial appearance as provided in G.S. 15A-511; and

(8)   To accept written appearances, waivers of trial and pleas of guilty in violations of G.S. 14-107 when the amount of the check is two thousand dollars ($2,000) or less, restitution, including service charges and processing fees allowed by G.S. 14-107, is made, and the warrant does not charge a fourth or subsequent violation of this statute, and in these cases to enter judgments as the chief district judge directs.

(9)   Repealed by Session Laws 1991 (Regular Session, 1992), c. 900, s. 118(d). (1965, c. 310, s. 1; 1969, c. 876, s. 2; c. 1190, s. 25; 1973, c. 6; c. 503, s. 8; c. 1286, s. 7; 1975, c. 626, s. 4; 1977, c. 873, s. 1; 1979, c. 144, s. 3; 1981, c. 555, s. 3; 1983, c. 586, s. 5; 1985, c. 425, s. 4; c. 764, s. 16; 1985 (Reg. Sess., 1986), c. 852, s. 17; 1987, c. 355, ss. 1, 2; 1989, c. 343; c. 763; 1989 (Reg. Sess., 1990), c. 1041, s. 1; 1991, c. 520, s. 2; 1991 (Reg. Sess., 1992), c. 900, s. 118(d); 1993, c. 374, s. 4; c. 538, s. 35; 1994, Ex. Sess., c. 14, s. 1; c. 24, s. 14(b); 1999-80, s. 1; 2002-159, s. 1.)

§ 7A-274. Power of mayors, law-enforcement officers, etc., to issue warrants and set bail restricted.

The power of mayors, law-enforcement officers, and other persons not officers of the General Court of Justice to issue arrest, search, or peace warrants, or to set bail, is terminated in any district court district upon the establishment of a district court therein. (1965, c. 310, s. 1.)

§ 7A-275. Repealed by Session Laws 1971, c. 377, s. 32.

§ 7A-276. Reserved for future codification purposes.

Article 22A.

Prohibited Orders.

§ 7A-276.1. Court orders prohibiting publication or broadcast of reports of open court proceedings or reports of public records banned.

No court shall make or issue any rule or order banning, prohibiting, or restricting the publication or broadcast of any report concerning any of the following: any evidence, testimony, argument, ruling, verdict, decision, judgment, or other matter occurring in open court in any hearing, trial, or other proceeding, civil or criminal; and no court shall issue any rule or order sealing, prohibiting, restricting the publication or broadcast of the contents of any public record as defined by any statute of this State, which is required to be open to public inspection under any valid statute, regulation, or rule of common law. If any rule or order is made or issued by any court in violation of the provisions of this statute, it shall be null and void and of no effect, and no person shall be punished for contempt for the violation of any such void rule or order. (1977, c. 711, s. 3.)

Article 23.

Jurisdiction and Procedure Applicable to Children.

§§ 7A-277 through 7A-289: Repealed by Session Laws 1979, c. 815, s. 1.

Article 24.

Juvenile Services.

§§ 7A-289.1 through 7A-289.6: Repealed by Session Laws 1998-202, s. 1(a).

§ 7A-289.7: Repealed by Session Laws 1979, c. 815, s. 1.

§§ 7A-289.8 through 7A-289.12: Reserved for future codification purposes.

Article 24A.

Delinquency Prevention and Youth Services.

§§ 7A-289.13 through 7A-289.16: Repealed by Session Laws 1998-202, s. 1(a).

§§ 7A-289.17 through 7A-289.21: Reserved for future codification purposes.

63

Article 24B.

Termination of Parental Rights.

§§ 7A-289.22 through 7A-289.23. Repealed by Session Laws 1998-202, s. 5.

§ 7A-289.23A. Recodified as § 7B-1102.

§§ 7A-289.24 through 7A-289.35: Repealed by Session Laws 1998-202, s. 5.

Article 25.

Jurisdiction and Procedure in Criminal Appeals from District Courts.

§ 7A-290. Appeals from district court in criminal cases; notice; appeal bond.

Any defendant convicted in district court before the magistrate may appeal to the district court for trial de novo before the district court judge. Any defendant convicted in district court before the judge may appeal to the superior court for trial de novo. Notice of appeal may be given orally in open court, or to the clerk in writing within 10 days of entry of judgment. Upon expiration of the 10-day period in which an appeal may be entered, if an appeal has been entered and not withdrawn, the clerk shall transfer the case to the district or superior court docket. The original bail shall stand pending appeal, unless the judge orders bail denied, increased, or reduced. (1965, c. 310, s. 1; 1967, c. 601, s. 1; 1969, c. 876, s. 3; c. 911, s. 5; c. 1190, s. 26; 1971, c. 377, s. 16.)

Article 26.

Additional Powers of District Court Judges and Magistrates.

§ 7A-291. Additional powers of district court judges.

In addition to the jurisdiction and powers assigned in this Chapter, a district court judge has the following powers:

(1)   To administer oaths;

64

(2)   To punish for contempt;

(3)   To compel the attendance of witnesses and the production of evidence;

(4)   To set bail;

(5)   To issue arrest warrants valid throughout the State, and search warrants valid throughout the district of issue; and

(6)   To issue all process and orders necessary or proper in the exercise of his powers and authority, and to effectuate his lawful judgments and decrees. (1965, c. 310, s. 1; 1969, c. 1190, s. 27; 1973, c. 1286, s. 11.)

§ 7A-292. Additional powers of magistrates.

In addition to the jurisdiction and powers assigned in this Chapter to the magistrate in civil and criminal actions, each magistrate has the following additional powers:

(1)   To administer oaths.

(2)   To punish for direct criminal contempt subject to the limitations contained in Chapter 5A of the General Statutes of North Carolina.

(3)   When authorized by the chief district judge, to take depositions and examinations before trial.

(4)   To issue subpoenas and capiases valid throughout the county.

(5)   To take affidavits for the verification of pleadings.

(6)   To issue writs of habeas corpus ad testificandum, as provided in G.S. 17-41.

(7)   To assign a year's allowance to the surviving spouse and a child's allowance to the children as provided in Chapter 30, Article 4, of the General Statutes.

(8)   To take acknowledgments of instruments, as provided in G.S. 47-1.

(9)   To perform the marriage ceremony, as provided in G.S. 51-1.

(10)   To take acknowledgment of a written contract or separation agreement between husband and wife.

(11)   Repealed by Session Laws 1973, c. 503, s. 9.

(12)   To assess contribution for damages or for work done on a dam, canal, or ditch, as provided in G.S. 156-15.

(13)   Repealed by Session Laws 1973, c. 503, s. 9.

(14)   To accept the filing of complaints and to issue summons pursuant to Article 4 of Chapter 42A of the General Statutes in expedited eviction proceedings when the office of the clerk of superior court is closed.

(15)   When authorized by the chief district judge, as permitted in G.S. 7A-146(11), to provide for appointment of counsel pursuant to Article 36 of this Chapter.

(16)   To appoint an umpire to determine motor vehicle liability policy diminution in value, as provided in G.S. 20-279.21(d1). (1965, c. 310, s. 1; 1967, c. 691, s. 25; 1971, c. 377, s. 17; 1973, c. 503, s. 9; 1977, c. 375, s. 4; 1979, 2nd Sess., c. 1080, s. 6; 1994, Ex. Sess., c. 4, s. 4; 1999-420, s. 4; 1999-456, s. 9(a), (b); 2009-419, s. 1; 2009-440, s. 2; 2009-566, s. 28; 2009-570, s. 48.2.)

§ 7A-293. Special authority of a magistrate assigned to a municipality located in more than one county of a district court district.

A magistrate assigned to an incorporated municipality, the boundaries of which lie in more than one county of a district court district, may, in criminal matters, exercise the powers granted by G.S. 7A-273 as if the corporate limits plus the territory embraced within a distance of one mile in all directions therefrom were located wholly within the magistrate's county of residence. Appeals from a magistrate exercising the authority granted by this section shall be taken in the district court in the county in which the offense was committed. A magistrate exercising the special authority granted by this section shall transmit all records, reports, and monies collected to the clerk of the superior court of the county in which the offense was committed. In addition, if a magistrate is assigned to an incorporated municipality, the boundaries of which lie in two or more district court districts, the magistrate may exercise the powers described in this section as if the counties were in the same district court district, if the clerks of superior court and the chief district court judges serving the districts in which the municipality is located agree in writing that the exercise of this special authority would promote the administration of justice in the municipality and in the districts. However, if a magistrate is assigned to an incorporated municipality, the boundaries of which lie in four or more counties, each of which is in a separate district court district, the magistrate may exercise the powers described in this section as if all the counties were in the same district court district, without the necessity of such an agreement between the clerks and judges of the affected counties, and the records, reports, and monies collected in connection with the exercise of that authority shall be transmitted to the clerk of the superior court district for the county in which the offense was committed. (1967, c. 691, s. 26; 1989, c. 795, s. 23(c1); 2009-398, s. 2.)

§§ 7A-294 through 7A-299: Reserved for future codification purposes.

SUBCHAPTER VI. REVENUES AND EXPENSES OF THE JUDICIAL DEPARTMENT.

Article 27.

Expenses of the Judicial Department.

§ 7A-300. Expenses paid from State funds.

(a)   The operating expenses of the Judicial Department shall be paid from State funds, out of appropriations for this purpose made by the General Assembly, or from funds provided by local governments pursuant to G.S. 7A-300.1, 153A-212.1, or 160A-289.1. The Administrative Office of the Courts shall prepare budget estimates to cover these expenses, including therein the following items and such other items as are deemed necessary for the proper functioning of the Judicial Department:

(1)   Salaries, departmental expense, printing and other costs of the appellate division;

(2)   Salaries and expenses of superior court judges, district attorneys, assistant district attorneys, public defenders, and assistant public defenders, and fees and expenses of counsel assigned to represent indigents under the provisions of Subchapter IX of this Chapter;

(3)   Salaries, travel expenses, departmental expense, printing and other costs of the Administrative Office of the Courts;

(4)   Salaries and travel expenses of district judges, magistrates, and family court counselors;

(5)   Salaries and travel expenses of clerks of superior court, their assistants, deputies, and other employees, and the expenses of their offices, including supplies and materials, postage, telephone and telegraph, bonds and insurance, equipment, and other necessary items;

(6)   Fees and travel expenses of jurors, and of witnesses required to be paid by the State;

(7)   Compensation and allowances of court reporters;

(8)   Briefs for counsel and transcripts and other records for adequate appellate review when an appeal is taken by an indigent person;

(9)   Transcripts of preliminary hearings in indigency cases and, in cases in which the defendant pays for a transcript of the preliminary hearing, a copy for the district attorney;

(10)   Transcript of the evidence and trial court charge furnished the district attorney when a criminal action is appealed to the appellate division;

(11)   All other expenses arising out of the operations of the Judicial Department which by law are made the responsibility of the State; and
(12)   Operating expenses of the Judicial Council and the Judicial Standards Commission.

(b)   Repealed by Session Laws 1971, c. 377, s. 32. (1965, c. 310, s. 1; 1967, c. 108, s. 9; c. 1049, s. 5; 1969, c. 1013, s. 2; 1971, c. 377, ss. 18, 21; 1973, c. 47, s. 2; c. 503, ss. 10, 11; 2000-67, s. 15.4(c); 2010-31, s. 29.7(a).)

§ 7A-300.1. Local supplementation of salaries for certain officers and employees.

(a)   In order to attract and retain the best qualified officers and employees for positions in the Judicial Branch of government, the Administrative Office of the Courts may contract with the governing body of a city or county for the provision of local funds to supplement the salaries of Judicial Department employees, other than elected officials and magistrates, who serve the superior court district, district court district, or prosecutorial district containing that unit of local government. Any employee who receives salary supplementation under this section shall be notified before receiving it that the supplementation is subject to the availability of local funds, may be discontinued at any time, and is not "compensation" for purposes of the Teachers' and State Employees' Retirement System or the Consolidated Judicial Retirement System.

(b)   This section applies only to (i) cities with a population of 300,000 or more according to the most recent estimate of the Office of State Budget and Management and (ii) counties with a population of 300,000 or over according to the most recent estimate of the Office of State Budget and Management. (2010-31, s. 29.7(b).)

§ 7A-301. Disbursement of expenses.

The salaries and expenses of all personnel in the Judicial Department and other operating expenses shall be paid out of the State treasury upon warrants duly drawn thereon, except that the Administrative Office of the Courts and the Department of Administration, with the approval of the State Auditor, may establish alternative procedures for the prompt payment of juror fees, witness fees, and other small expense items. (1965, c. 310, s. 1.)

§ 7A-302. Counties and municipalities responsible for physical facilities.

In each county in which a district court has been established, courtrooms, office space for juvenile court counselors and support staff as assigned by the Division of Juvenile Justice of the Department of Public Safety, and related judicial facilities (including furniture), as defined in this Subchapter, shall be provided by the county, except that courtrooms and related judicial facilities may, with the approval of the administrative Officer of the Courts, after consultation with county and municipal authorities, be provided by a municipality in the county. To

69

assist a county or municipality in meeting the expense of providing courtrooms and related judicial facilities, a part of the costs of court, known as the "facilities fee," collected for the State by the clerk of superior court, shall be remitted to the county or municipality providing the facilities. (1965, c. 310, s. 1; 1998-202, s. 15; 2000-137, s. 4(a); 2007-323, s. 14.16; 2008-107, s. 29.8(f); 2011-145, s. 19.1(l).)

§ 7A-303. Equipment and supplies in clerk's office.

Upon the establishment of the district court in any county, supplies and all equipment in the office of the clerk of superior court shall become the property of the State. (1965, c. 310, s. 1.)

Article 28.

Uniform Costs and Fees in the Trial Divisions.

§ 7A-304. Costs in criminal actions.

(a)   In every criminal case in the superior or district court, wherein the defendant is convicted, or enters a plea of guilty or nolo contendere, or when costs are assessed against the prosecuting witness, the following costs shall be assessed and collected. No costs may be assessed when a case is dismissed. Only upon entry of a written order, supported by findings of fact and conclusions of law, determining that there is just cause, the court may (i) waive costs assessed under this section or (ii) waive or reduce costs assessed under subdivision (7), (8), (11), or (12) of this section.

(1)   For each arrest or personal service of criminal process, including citations and subpoenas, the sum of five dollars ($5.00), to be remitted to the county wherein the arrest was made or process was served, except that in those cases in which the arrest was made or process served by a law-enforcement officer employed by a municipality, the fee shall be paid to the municipality employing the officer.

(2)   For the use of the courtroom and related judicial facilities, the sum of twelve dollars ($12.00) in the district court, including cases before a magistrate, and the sum of thirty dollars ($30.00) in superior court, to be remitted to the

county in which the judgment is rendered. In all cases where the judgment is rendered in facilities provided by a municipality, the facilities fee shall be paid to the municipality. Funds derived from the facilities fees shall be used exclusively by the county or municipality for providing, maintaining, and constructing adequate courtroom and related judicial facilities, including: adequate space and furniture for judges, district attorneys, public defenders and other personnel of the Office of Indigent Defense Services, magistrates, juries, and other court related personnel; office space, furniture and vaults for the clerk; jail and juvenile detention facilities; free parking for jurors; and a law library (including books) if one has heretofore been established or if the governing body hereafter decides to establish one. In the event the funds derived from the facilities fees exceed what is needed for these purposes, the county or municipality may use any or all of the excess to retire outstanding indebtedness incurred in the construction of the facilities, or to reimburse the county or municipality for funds expended in constructing or renovating the facilities (without incurring any indebtedness) within a period of two years before or after the date a district court is established in such county, or to supplement the operations of the General Court of Justice in the county.

(2a)   For the upgrade, maintenance, and operation of the judicial and county courthouse phone systems, the sum of four dollars ($4.00), to be credited to the Court Information Technology Fund.

(2b)   For the maintenance of misdemeanors in county jails, the sum of eighteen dollars ($18.00) in the district court to be remitted to the Statewide Misdemeanor Confinement Fund in the Division of Adult Correction of the Department of Public Safety.

(3)   For the retirement and insurance benefits of both State and local government law-enforcement officers, the sum of six dollars and twenty-five cents ($6.25), to be remitted to the State Treasurer. Fifty cents (50¢) of this sum shall be administered as is provided in Article 12C of Chapter 143 of the General Statutes. Five dollars and seventy-five cents ($5.75) of this sum shall be administered as is provided in Article 12E of Chapter 143 of the General Statutes, with one dollar and twenty-five cents ($1.25) being administered in accordance with the provisions of G.S. 143-166.50(e).

(3a)   For the supplemental pension benefits of sheriffs, the sum of one dollar twenty-five cents ($1.25) to be remitted to the Department of Justice and administered under the provisions of Article 12H of Chapter 143 of the General Statutes.

(3b)   For the services, staffing, and operations of the Criminal Justice Education and Standards Commission, the sum of two dollars ($2.00) to be remitted to the Department of Justice.

(4)   For support of the General Court of Justice, the sum of one hundred twenty-nine dollars and fifty cents ($129.50) in the district court, including cases before a magistrate, and the sum of one hundred fifty-four dollars and fifty cents ($154.50) in the superior court, to be remitted to the State Treasurer. For a person convicted of a felony in superior court who has made a first appearance in district court, both the district court and superior court fees shall be assessed. The State Treasurer shall remit the sum of one dollar and fifty cents ($1.50) of each fee collected under this subdivision to the North Carolina State Bar for the provision of services described in G.S. 7A-474.4, and ninety-five cents ($.95) of each fee collected under this subdivision to the North Carolina State Bar for the provision of services described in G.S. 7A-474.19.

(4a)   For support of the General Court of Justice, the sum of ten dollars ($10.00) for all offenses arising under Chapter 20 of the General Statutes, to be remitted to the State Treasurer.

(4b)   To provide for contractual services to reduce county jail populations, the sum of fifty dollars ($50.00) for all offenses arising under Chapter 20 of the General Statutes and resulting in a conviction of an improper equipment offense, to be remitted to the Statewide Misdemeanor Confinement Fund in the Division of Adult Correction of the Department of Public Safety.

(5)   For using pretrial release services, the district or superior court judge shall, upon conviction, impose a fee of fifteen dollars ($15.00) to be remitted to the county providing the pretrial release services. This cost shall be assessed and collected only if the defendant had been accepted and released to the supervision of the agency providing the pretrial release services.

(6)   For support of the General Court of Justice, the sum of two hundred dollars ($200.00) is payable by a defendant who fails to appear to answer the charge as scheduled, unless within 20 days after the scheduled appearance, the person either appears in court to answer the charge or disposes of the charge pursuant to G.S. 7A-146, and the sum of fifty dollars ($50.00) is payable by a defendant who fails to pay a fine, penalty, or costs within 20 days of the date specified in the court's judgment. Upon a showing to the court that the defendant failed to appear because of an error or omission of a judicial official, a

72

prosecutor, or a law-enforcement officer, the court shall waive the fee for failure to appear. These fees shall be remitted to the State Treasurer.

(7)   For the services of the North Carolina State Crime Laboratory facilities, the district or superior court judge shall, upon conviction, order payment of the sum of six hundred dollars ($600.00) to be remitted to the Department of Justice for support of the Laboratory. This cost shall be assessed only in cases in which, as part of the investigation leading to the defendant's conviction, the laboratories have performed DNA analysis of the crime, tests of bodily fluids of the defendant for the presence of alcohol or controlled substances, or analysis of any controlled substance possessed by the defendant or the defendant's agent.

(8)   For the services of any crime laboratory facility operated by a local government or group of local governments, the district or superior court judge shall, upon conviction, order payment of the sum of six hundred dollars ($600.00) to be remitted to the general fund of the local governmental unit that operates the laboratory to be used for law enforcement purposes. The cost shall be assessed only in cases in which, as part of the investigation leading to the defendant's conviction, the laboratory has performed DNA analysis of the crime, test of bodily fluids of the defendant for the presence of alcohol or controlled substances, or analysis of any controlled substance possessed by the defendant or the defendant's agent. The costs shall be assessed only if the court finds that the work performed at the local government's laboratory is the equivalent of the same kind of work performed by the North Carolina State Crime Laboratory under subdivision (7) of this subsection.

(9)   For the support and services of the State DNA Database and DNA Databank, the sum of two dollars ($2.00). This amount is annually appropriated to the Department of Justice for this purpose. Notwithstanding the provisions of subsection (e) of this section, this cost does not apply to infractions.

(10)   For support of the General Court of Justice, the sum of one hundred dollars ($100.00) is payable by a defendant convicted under G.S. 20-138.1 or G.S. 20-138.2, for a second or subsequent conviction under G.S. 20-138.2A, or for a second or subsequent conviction under G.S. 20-138.2B, to be remitted to the State Treasurer. This fee shall be in addition to the fee required by subdivision (4a) of this subsection.

(11)   For the services of an expert witness employed by the North Carolina State Crime Laboratory who completes a chemical analysis pursuant to G.S. 20-

139.1 or a forensic analysis pursuant to G.S. 8-58.20 and provides testimony about that analysis in a defendant's trial, the district or superior court judge shall, upon conviction of the defendant, order payment of the sum of six hundred dollars ($600.00) to be remitted to the Department of Justice for support of the State Crime Laboratory. This cost shall be assessed only in cases in which the expert witness provides testimony about the chemical or forensic analysis in the defendant's trial and shall be in addition to any cost assessed under subdivision (7) of this subsection.

(12)   For the services of an expert witness employed by a crime laboratory operated by a local government or group of local governments who completes a chemical analysis pursuant to G.S. 20-139.1 or a forensic analysis pursuant to G.S. 8-58.20 and provides testimony about that analysis in a defendant's trial, the district or superior court judge shall, upon conviction of the defendant, order payment of the sum of six hundred dollars ($600.00) to be remitted to the general fund of the local governmental unit that operates the laboratory to be used for local law enforcement. This cost shall be assessed only in cases in which the expert witness provides testimony about the chemical or forensic analysis in the defendant's trial and shall be in addition to any cost assessed under subdivision (8) of this subsection.

(a1)   Repealed by Session Laws 1997-475, s. 4.1.

(b)   On appeal, costs are cumulative, and costs assessed before a magistrate shall be added to costs assessed in the district court, and costs assessed in the district court shall be added to costs assessed in the superior court, except that the fee for the Law-Enforcement Officers' Benefit and Retirement Fund and the Sheriffs' Supplemental Pension Fund and the fee for pretrial release services shall be assessed only once in each case. No superior court costs shall be assessed against a defendant who gives notice of appeal from the district court but withdraws it prior to the expiration of the 10-day period for entering notice of appeal. When a case is reversed on appeal, the defendant shall not be liable for costs, and the State shall be liable for the cost of printing records and briefs in the Appellate Division.

(c)   Witness fees, expenses for blood tests and comparisons incurred by G.S. 8-50.1(a), jail fees and cost of necessary trial transcripts shall be assessed as provided by law in addition to other costs set out in this section. Nothing in this section shall limit the power or discretion of the judge in imposing fines or forfeitures or ordering restitution.

(d) (1) In any criminal case in which the liability for costs, fines, restitution, attorneys' fees, or any other lawful charge has been finally determined, the clerk of superior court shall, unless otherwise ordered by the presiding judge, disburse such funds when paid in accordance with the following priorities:

a. Sums in restitution to the victim entitled thereto;

b. Costs due the county;

c. Costs due the city;

d. Fines to the county school fund;

e. Sums in restitution prorated among the persons other than the victim entitled thereto;

f. Costs due the State;

g. Attorney's fees, including appointment fees assessed pursuant to G.S. 7A-455.1.

(2) Sums in restitution received by the clerk of superior court shall be disbursed when:

a. Complete restitution has been received; or

b. When, in the opinion of the clerk, additional payments in restriction will not be collected; or
c. Upon the request of the person or persons entitled thereto; and

d. In any event, at least once each calendar year.

(e) Unless otherwise provided by law, the costs assessed pursuant to this section for criminal actions disposed of in the district court are also applicable to infractions disposed of in the district court. The costs assessed in superior court for criminal actions appealed from district court to superior court are also applicable to infractions appealed to superior court. If an infraction is disposed of in the superior court pursuant to G.S. 7A-271(d), costs applicable to the original charge are applicable to the infraction.

(f)   The court may allow a defendant owing monetary obligations under this
section to either make payment in full when costs are assessed or make
payment on an installment plan arranged with the court. Defendants making use
of an installment plan shall pay a onetime setup fee of twenty dollars ($20.00) to
cover the additional costs to the court of receiving and disbursing installment
payments. Fees collected under this subsection shall be remitted to the State
Treasurer for support of the General Court of Justice.

(g)   Changes to the costs or fees in this section apply to costs or fees
assessed or collected on or after the effective date of the change. However, in
misdemeanor or infraction cases disposed of on or after the effective date by
written appearance, waiver of trial or hearing, or plea of guilt or admission of
responsibility pursuant to G.S. 7A-180(4) or G.S. 7A-273(2), and within the time
limit imposed by G.S. 7A-304(a)(6), in which the citation or other criminal
process was issued before the effective date, the costs or fees shall be the
lesser of those specified in this section as amended, or those specified in the
notice portion of the defendant's or respondent's copy of the citation or other
criminal process, if any costs or fees are specified in that notice. (1965, c. 310,
s. 1; 1967, c. 601, s. 2; c. 691, ss. 27-29; c. 1049, s. 5; 1969, c. 1013, s. 3; c.
1190, ss. 28, 29; 1971, c. 377, ss. 19-21; c. 1129; 1973, c. 47, s. 2; 1975, c.
558, ss. 1, 2; 1975, 2nd Sess., c. 980, s. 1; 1979, c. 576, s. 3; 1981, c. 369; c.
691, s. 1; c. 896, s. 2; c. 959, s. 1; 1983, c. 713, ss. 2, 3; 1983 (Reg. Sess.,
1984), c. 1034, s. 249; 1985, c. 479, s. 196(a); c. 729, ss. 2-4; c. 764, s. 17;
1986, Ex. Sess., c. 5; 1985 (Reg. Sess., 1986), c. 852, s. 17; c. 1015, s. 1;
1989, c. 664, ss. 1, 2; c. 786, s. 1; 1989 (Reg. Sess., 1990), c. 1044, s. 1; 1991,
c. 742, s. 15(a); 1991 (Reg. Sess., 1992), c. 811, s. 1; 1993, c. 313, s. 2; 1996,
2nd Ex. Sess., c. 18, s. 22.13(a); 1997-475, s. 4.1; 1998-212, ss. 19.4(k),
29A.12(a); 2000-109, s. 4(a); 2000-144, s. 2; 2001-424, s. 22.14(a); 2002-126,
ss. 29A.4(a), 29A.8(a), 29A.9(b); 2003-284, s. 30.19B(a); 2004-186, s. 4.4;
2005-250, s. 1; 2005-276, ss. 43.1(a), 29.30(b); 2005-363, s. 1; 2007-323, s.
30.8(a); 2008-107, s. 29.8(a); 2008-118, s. 2.9(a); 2009-451, s. 15.20(a), (b),
(c); 2009-516, s. 1; 2009-575, s. 13A; 2010-31, s. 15.5(a); 2010-123, s. 6.1;
2010-147, s. 7.1; 2011-19, s. 5; 2011-145, ss. 15.10(a), 19.1(h), 31.23(a),
31.23B, 31.26(b), (c), 31.26A; 2011-191, s. 4; 2011-192, s. 7(n), (o); 2011-326,
s. 2; 2011-391, ss. 63(a), (b), 66; 2012-142, ss. 16.5(b), 16.6(b); 2013-360, ss.
17.6(g), 18B.18(a), 18B.19(a).)

§ 7A-305. Costs in civil actions.

(a)   In every civil action in the superior or district court, except for actions brought under Chapter 50B of the General Statutes, shall be assessed:

(1)   For the use of the courtroom and related judicial facilities, the sum of twelve dollars ($12.00) in cases heard before a magistrate, and the sum of sixteen dollars ($16.00) in district and superior court, to be remitted to the county in which the judgment is rendered, except that in all cases in which the judgment is rendered in facilities provided by a municipality, the facilities fee shall be paid to the municipality. Funds derived from the facilities fees shall be used in the same manner, for the same purposes, and subject to the same restrictions, as facilities fees assessed in criminal actions.

(1a)   For the upgrade, maintenance, and operation of the judicial and county courthouse phone systems, the sum of four dollars ($4.00), to be credited to the Court Information Technology Fund.

(2)   For support of the General Court of Justice, the sum of one hundred eighty dollars ($180.00) in the superior court and the sum of one hundred thirty dollars ($130.00) in the district court except that if the case is assigned to a magistrate the sum shall be eighty dollars ($80.00). If a case is assigned to a special superior court judge as a complex business case under G.S. 7A-45.3, upon assignment the party filing the notice of designation pursuant to G.S. 7A-45.4 or the motion for complex business designation shall pay an additional one thousand dollars ($1,000) for support of the General Court of Justice; if a case is assigned to a special superior court judge as a complex business case under G.S. 7A-45.3 by a court on its own motion, upon assignment the plaintiff shall pay an additional one thousand dollars ($1,000) for support of the General Court of Justice. Sums collected under this subdivision shall be remitted to the State Treasurer. The State Treasurer shall remit the sum of one dollar and fifty cents ($1.50) of each fee collected under this subdivision to the North Carolina State Bar for the provision of services described in G.S. 7A-474.4, and ninety-five cents ($.95) of each fee collected under this subdivision to the North Carolina State Bar for the provision of services described in G.S. 7A-474.19.

(a1)   Costs apply to any and all additional and subsequent actions filed by amendment or counterclaim to the original action brought under Chapter 50B of the General Statutes, unless such additional and subsequent amendment or counterclaim to the action is limited to requests for relief authorized by Chapter 50B of the General Statutes.

(a2) (Effective until July 1, 2014) In every action for absolute divorce filed in the district court, a cost of seventy-five dollars ($75.00) shall be assessed against the person filing the divorce action. Costs collected by the clerk pursuant to this subsection shall be remitted to the State Treasurer, who shall deposit thirty-five dollars ($35.00) to the North Carolina Fund for Displaced Homemakers established under G.S. 143B-394.10 and forty dollars ($40.00) to the Domestic Violence Center Fund established under G.S. 50B-9. Costs assessed under this subsection shall be in addition to any other costs assessed under this section.

(a2) (Effective July 1, 2014) In every action for absolute divorce filed in the district court, a cost of seventy-five dollars ($75.00) shall be assessed against the person filing the divorce action. Costs collected by the clerk pursuant to this subsection shall be remitted to the State Treasurer, who shall deposit seventy-five dollars ($75.00) to the Domestic Violence Center Fund established under G.S. 50B-9. Costs assessed under this subsection shall be in addition to any other costs assessed under this section.

(a3), (a4) Repealed by Session Laws 2008-118, s. 2.9(c), effective July 1, 2008.

(a5) In every civil action in the superior or district court wherein a party files a pleading containing one or more counterclaims, third-party complaints, or cross-claims, except for counterclaim and cross-claim actions brought under Chapter 50B of the General Statutes for which costs are assessed pursuant to subsection (a1) of this section, the following shall be assessed:

(1) For the use of the courtroom and related judicial facilities, the sum of twelve dollars ($12.00) in cases heard before a magistrate, and the sum of sixteen dollars ($16.00) in district and superior court, to be remitted to the municipality providing the facilities in which the judgment is rendered. If a municipality does not provide the facilities in which the judgment is rendered, the sum is to be remitted to the county in which the judgment is rendered. Funds derived from the facilities' fees shall be used in the same manner, for the same purposes, and subject to the same restrictions as facilities' fees assessed in criminal actions.

(2) For the upgrade, maintenance, and operation of the judicial and county courthouse phone systems, the sum of four dollars ($4.00), to be credited to the Court Information Technology Fund.

(3)   For support of the General Court of Justice, the sum of one hundred eighty dollars ($180.00) in the superior court, except that if a case is assigned to a special superior court judge as a complex business case under G.S. 7A-45.3, filing fees shall be collected and disbursed in accordance with subsection (a) of this section, and the sum of one hundred thirty dollars ($130.00) in the district court, except that if the case is assigned to a magistrate, the sum shall be eighty dollars ($80.00). Sums collected under this subdivision shall be remitted to the State Treasurer. The State Treasurer shall remit the sum of one dollar and fifty cents ($1.50) of each fee collected under this subdivision to the North Carolina State Bar for the provision of services described in G.S. 7A-474.4, and ninety-five cents ($.95) of each fee collected under this subdivision to the North Carolina State Bar for the provision of services described in G.S. 7A-474.19.

(b)   On appeal, costs are cumulative, and when cases heard before a magistrate are appealed to the district court, the General Court of Justice fee and the facilities fee applicable in the district court shall be added to the fees assessed before the magistrate. When an order of the clerk of the superior court is appealed to either the district court or the superior court, no additional General Court of Justice fee or facilities fee shall be assessed.

(b1)   When a defendant files an answer in an action filed as a small claim which requires the entire case to be withdrawn from a magistrate and transferred to the district court, the difference between the General Court of Justice fee and facilities fee applicable to the district court and the General Court of Justice fee and facilities fee applicable to cases heard by a magistrate shall be assessed. The defendant is responsible for paying the fee.

(c)   The clerk of superior court, at the time of the filing of the papers initiating the action or the appeal, shall collect as advance court costs, the facilities fee, General Court of Justice fee, and the divorce fee imposed under subsection (a2) of this section, except in suits by an indigent. The clerk shall also collect the fee for discovery procedures under Rule 27(a) and (b) at the time of the filing of the verified petition.

(d)   The following expenses, when incurred, are assessable or recoverable, as the case may be. The expenses set forth in this subsection are complete and exclusive and constitute a limit on the trial court's discretion to tax costs pursuant to G.S. 6-20:

(1)   Witness fees, as provided by law.

79

(2)   Jail fees, as provided by law.

(3)   Counsel fees, as provided by law.

(4)   Expense of service of process by certified mail and by publication.

(5)   Costs on appeal to the superior court, or to the appellate division, as the case may be, of the original transcript of testimony, if any, insofar as essential to the appeal.

(6)   Fees for personal service and civil process and other sheriff's fees, as provided by law. Fees for personal service by a private process server may be recoverable in an amount equal to the actual cost of such service or fifty dollars ($50.00), whichever is less, unless the court finds that due to difficulty of service a greater amount is appropriate.

(7)   Fees of mediators appointed by the court, mediators agreed upon by the parties, guardians ad litem, referees, receivers, commissioners, surveyors, arbitrators, appraisers, and other similar court appointees, as provided by law. The fee of such appointees shall include reasonable reimbursement for stenographic assistance, when necessary.

(8)   Fees of interpreters, when authorized and approved by the court.

(9)   Premiums for surety bonds for prosecution, as authorized by G.S. 1-109.

(10)   Reasonable and necessary expenses for stenographic and videographic assistance directly related to the taking of depositions and for the cost of deposition transcripts.

(11)   Reasonable and necessary fees of expert witnesses solely for actual time spent providing testimony at trial, deposition, or other proceedings.

Nothing in this subsection or in G.S. 6-20 shall be construed to limit the trial court's authority to award fees and expenses in connection with pretrial discovery matters as provided in Rule 26(b) or Rule 37 of the Rules of Civil Procedure, and no award of costs made pursuant to this section or pursuant to G.S. 6-20 shall reverse or modify any such orders entered in connection with pretrial discovery.

80

(e)   Nothing in this section shall affect the liability of the respective parties for costs as provided by law.

(f)   For the support of the General Court of Justice, the sum of twenty dollars ($20.00) shall accompany any filing of a notice of hearing on a motion not listed in G.S. 7A-308 that is filed with the clerk. No costs shall be assessed to a notice of hearing on a motion containing as a sole claim for relief the taxing of costs, including attorneys' fees, to a motion filed pursuant to G.S. 1C-1602 or G.S. 1C-1603, or to a motion filed by a child support enforcement agency established pursuant to Part D of Title IV of the Social Security Act. No more than one fee shall be assessed for any motion for which a notice of hearing is filed, regardless of whether the hearing is continued, rescheduled, or otherwise delayed. (1965, c. 310, s. 1; 1967, c. 108, s. 10; c. 691, s. 30; 1971, c. 377, ss. 23, 24; c. 1181, s. 1; 1973, c. 503, ss. 12-14; c. 1267, s. 3; 1975, c. 558, s. 3; 1975, 2nd Sess., c. 980, ss. 2, 3; 1979, 2nd Sess., c. 1234, s. 1; 1981, c. 555, s. 6; c. 691, s. 2; 1983, c. 713, ss. 4-6; 1989, c. 786, s. 2; 1991, c. 742, s. 15(b); 1991 (Reg. Sess., 1992), c. 811, s. 2; 1993, c. 435, s. 6; 1995, c. 275, s. 2; 1998-212, s. 29A.12(b); 1998-219, ss. 2, 3; 2000-109, s. 4(b); 2001-424, s. 22.14(b); 2002-126, ss. 29A.4(b), 29A.6(e); 2004-186, s. 4.3; 2005-276, s. 43.1(b); 2005-405, s. 5; 2005-425, s. 1.2; 2007-212, s. 3; 2007-293, s. 2; 2007-323, ss. 30.8(b), 30.10(a), 30.11(a), (c); 2007-345, ss. 9.1(a), (c); 2008-107, ss. 29.1(a), 29.8(b); 2008-118, s. 2.9(c); 2008-193, s. 2; 2009-451, s. 15.20(d), (e); 2010-31, ss. 15.5(b), 15.8(a); 2010-123, s. 6.1; 2011-145, s. 31.23(b); 2012-142, s. 16.5(c); 2013-225, ss. 2, 3, 4(a); 2013-360, ss. 18B.17(a), 30.2(a), 30.2(a1); 2013-363, s. 7.1.)

§ 7A-305.1. Discovery, fee on filing verified petition.

When discovery procedures under Rule 27 of the Rules of Civil Procedure are utilized, the sum of twenty dollars ($20.00) shall be assessed and collected by the clerk at the time of the filing of the verified petition. If a civil action is subsequently initiated, the twenty dollars ($20.00) shall be credited against costs in the civil action. (1971, c. 377, s. 22.)

§ 7A-306. Costs in special proceedings.

(a)   In every special proceeding in the superior court, the following costs shall be assessed:

(1)   For the use of the courtroom and related judicial facilities, the sum of ten dollars ($10.00) to be remitted to the county. Funds derived from the facilities fees shall be used in the same manner, for the same purposes, and subject to the same restrictions, as facilities fees assessed in criminal actions.

(1a)   For the upgrade, maintenance, and operation of the judicial and county courthouse phone systems, the sum of four dollars ($4.00), to be credited to the Court Information Technology Fund.

(2)   For support of the General Court of Justice the sum of one hundred six dollars ($106.00). In addition, in proceedings involving land, except boundary disputes, if the fair market value of the land involved is over one hundred dollars ($100.00), there shall be an additional sum of thirty cents (30¢) per one hundred dollars ($100.00) of value, or major fraction thereof, not to exceed a maximum additional sum of two hundred dollars ($200.00). Fair market value is determined by the sale price if there is a sale, the appraiser's valuation if there is no sale, or the appraised value from the property tax records if there is neither a sale nor an appraiser's valuation. Sums collected under this subdivision shall be remitted to the State Treasurer. The State Treasurer shall remit the sum of one dollar and fifty cents ($1.50) of each one hundred six-dollar ($106.00) General Court of Justice fee collected under this subdivision to the North Carolina State Bar for the provision of services described in G.S. 7A-474.4.

(b)   The facilities fee and thirty dollars ($30.00) of the General Court of Justice fee are payable at the time the proceeding is initiated.

(c)   The following additional expenses, when incurred, are assessable or recoverable, as the case may be:

(1)   Witness fees, as provided by law.

(2)   Counsel fees, as provided by law.

(3)   Costs on appeal, of the original transcript of testimony, if any, insofar as essential to the appeal.

(4)   Fees for personal service of civil process, and other sheriff's fees, and for service by publication, as provided by law.

(5)   Fees of guardians ad litem, referees, receivers, commissioners, surveyors, arbitrators, appraisers, and other similar court appointees, as

82

provided by law. The fees of such appointees shall include reasonable reimbursement for stenographic assistance, when necessary.

(d)   Costs assessed before the clerk shall be added to costs assessable on appeal to the judge or upon transfer to the civil issue docket.

(e)   Nothing in this section shall affect the liability of the respective parties for costs, as provided by law.

(f)   This section does not apply to a foreclosure under power of sale in a deed of trust or mortgage.

(g)   For the support of the General Court of Justice, the sum of twenty dollars ($20.00) shall accompany any filing of a notice of hearing on a motion not listed in G.S. 7A-308 that is filed with the clerk. No costs shall be assessed to a notice of hearing on a motion containing as a sole claim for relief the taxing of costs, including attorneys' fees, or to a motion filed pursuant to G.S. 1C-1602 or G.S. 1C-1603. No more than one fee shall be assessed for any motion for which a notice of hearing is filed, regardless of whether the hearing is continued, rescheduled, or otherwise delayed. (1965, c. 310, s. 1; 1967, c. 24, s. 2; 1971, c. 377, s. 25; c. 1181, s. 1; 1973, c. 503, s. 15; 1981, c. 691, s. 3; 1983, c. 713, ss. 7-9; c. 881, s. 4; 1985, c. 511, s. 1; 1989, c. 646, s. 1; 1991 (Reg. Sess., 1992), c. 811, s. 3; 1998-212, s. 29A.12(c); 2000-109, s. 4(c); 2001-424, s. 22.14(c); 2002-135, s. 1; 2005-276, s. 43.1(c); 2007-323, s. 30.8(c); 2008-107, s. 29.8(c); 2009-451, s. 15.20(f), (g); 2011-145, s. 31.23(c); 2012-142, s. 16.5(d); 2013-225, s. 4(b); 2013-360, s. 18B.17(b).)

§ 7A-307. Costs in administration of estates.

(a)   In the administration of the estates of decedents, minors, incompetents, of missing persons, and of trusts under wills and under powers of attorney, in trust proceedings under G.S. 36C-2-203, in estate proceedings under G.S. 28A-2-4, and in collections of personal property by affidavit, the following costs shall be assessed:

(1)   For the use of the courtroom and related judicial facilities, the sum of ten dollars ($10.00), to be remitted to the county. Funds derived from the facilities fees shall be used in the same manner, for the same purposes, and subject to the same restrictions, as facilities fees assessed in criminal actions.

83

(1a)   For the upgrade, maintenance, and operation of the judicial and county courthouse phone systems, the sum of four dollars ($4.00), to be credited to the Court Information Technology Fund.

(2)   For support of the General Court of Justice, the sum of one hundred six dollars ($106.00), plus an additional forty cents (40¢) per one hundred dollars ($100.00), or major fraction thereof, of the gross estate, not to exceed six thousand dollars ($6,000). Gross estate shall include the fair market value of all personalty when received, and all proceeds from the sale of realty coming into the hands of the fiduciary, but shall not include the value of realty. In collections of personal property by affidavit, the fee based on the gross estate shall be computed from the information in the final affidavit of collection made pursuant to G.S. 28A-25-3 and shall be paid when that affidavit is filed. In all other cases, this fee shall be computed from the information reported in the inventory and shall be paid when the inventory is filed with the clerk. If additional gross estate, including income, comes into the hands of the fiduciary after the filing of the inventory, the fee for such additional value shall be assessed and paid upon the filing of any account or report disclosing such additional value. For each filing the minimum fee shall be fifteen dollars ($15.00). Sums collected under this subdivision shall be remitted to the State Treasurer. The State Treasurer shall remit the sum of one dollar and fifty cents ($1.50) of each one hundred six-dollar ($106.00) General Court of Justice fee collected under this subdivision to the North Carolina State Bar for the provision of services described in G.S. 7A-474.4.

(2a)   Notwithstanding subdivision (2) of this subsection, the fee of forty cents (40¢) per one hundred dollars ($100.00), or major fraction, of the gross estate, not to exceed six thousand dollars ($6,000), shall not be assessed on personalty received by a trust under a will when the estate of the decedent was administered under Chapters 28 or 28A of the General Statutes. Instead, a fee of twenty dollars ($20.00) shall be assessed on the filing of each annual and final account. However, the fee shall be assessed only on newly contributed or acquired assets, all interest or other income that accrues or is earned on or with respect to any existing or newly contributed or acquired assets, and realized gains on the sale of any and all trust assets. Newly contributed or acquired assets do not include assets acquired by the sale, transfer, exchange, or otherwise of the amount of trust property on which fees were previously assessed.

(2b)   Notwithstanding subdivisions (1) and (2) of this subsection, no costs shall be assessed when the estate is administered or settled pursuant to G.S. 28A-25-6.

(2c)   Notwithstanding subdivision (2) of this subsection, the fee of forty cents (40¢) per one hundred dollars ($100.00), or major fraction, of the gross estate shall not be assessed on the gross estate of a trust that is the subject of a proceeding under G.S. 36C-2-203 if there is no requirement in the trust that accountings be filed with the clerk.

(2d)   Notwithstanding subdivisions (1) and (2) of this subsection, the only cost assessed in connection with the qualification of a limited personal representative under G.S. 28A-29-1 shall be a fee of twenty dollars ($20.00) to be assessed upon the filing of the petition.

(3)   For probate of a will without qualification of a personal representative, the clerk shall assess a facilities fee as provided in subdivision (1) of this subsection and shall assess for support of the General Court of Justice, the sum of twenty dollars ($20.00).

(4)   For the support of the General Court of Justice, the sum of twenty dollars ($20.00) shall accompany any filing of a notice of hearing on a motion not listed in G.S. 7A-308 that is filed with the clerk. No costs shall be assessed to a notice of hearing on a motion containing as a sole claim for relief the taxing of costs, including attorneys' fees, or to a motion filed pursuant to G.S. 1C-1602 or G.S. 1C-1603. No more than one fee shall be assessed for any motion for which a notice of hearing is filed, regardless of whether the hearing is continued, rescheduled, or otherwise delayed.

(5)   For the filing of a caveat to a will, the clerk shall assess for support of the General Court of Justice, the sum of two hundred dollars ($200.00).

(6)   Notwithstanding subdivisions (1) and (2) of this subsection, the only cost assessed in connection with the reopening of an estate administration under G.S. 28A-23-5 shall be forty cents (40¢) per one hundred dollars ($100.00), or major fraction, of any additional gross estate, including income, coming into the hands of the fiduciary after the estate is reopened; provided that the total cost assessed when added to the total cost assessed in all prior administrations of the estate shall not exceed six thousand dollars ($6,000).

(b)   In collections of personal property by affidavit, the facilities fee and thirty dollars ($30.00) of the General Court of Justice fee shall be paid at the time of filing the qualifying affidavit pursuant to G.S. 28A-25-1. In all other cases, these fees shall be paid at the time of filing of the first inventory. If the sole asset of the estate is a cause of action, these fees shall be paid at the time of the qualification of the fiduciary.

(b1)   The clerk shall assess the following miscellaneous fees:

(1)   Filing and indexing a will with no probate

        - first page.. $ 1.00

        - each additional page or fraction thereof.. .25

(2)   Issuing letters to fiduciaries, per letter over five letters issued................. 1.00

(3)   Inventory of safe deposits of a decedent, per box, per day.................... 15.00

(4)   Taking a deposition.. 10.00

(5)   Docketing and indexing a will probated in another county in the State

        - first page... 6.00

        - each additional page or fraction thereof.. .25

(6)   Hearing petition for year's allowance to surviving spouse or child, in cases not assigned to a magistrate, and allotting the same...................................... 8.00

(c)   The following additional expenses, when incurred, are also assessable or recoverable, as the case may be:

(1)   Witness fees, as provided by law.

(2)   Counsel fees, as provided by law.

(3)   Costs on appeal, of the original transcript of testimony, if any, insofar as essential to the appeal.

(4)   Fees for personal service of civil process, and other sheriff's fees, as provided by law.

(5)   Fees of guardians ad litem, referees, receivers, commissioners, surveyors, arbitrators, appraisers, and other similar court appointees, as provided by law.

(d)   Costs assessed before the clerk shall be added to costs assessable on appeal to the judge or upon transfer to the civil issue docket.

(e)   Nothing in this section shall affect the liability of the respective parties for costs, as provided by law. (1965, c. 310, s. 1; 1967, c. 691, s. 31; 1969, c. 1190, s. 30; 1971, c. 1181, s. 1; 1973, c. 1335, s. 1; 1981, c. 691, s. 4; 1983, c. 713, ss. 10-17; 1985, c. 481, ss. 1-5; 1985 (Reg. Sess., 1986), c. 855; 1987, c. 837; 1989, c. 719; 1991 (Reg. Sess., 1992), c. 811, ss. 4, 5; 1997-310, s. 4; 1998-212, s. 29A.12(d); 2000-109, s. 4(d); 2001-413, s. 1.2; 2001-424, s. 22.14(d); 2002-135, ss. 2, 3; 2005-276, s. 43.1(d); 2007-323, ss. 30.8(d), 30.10(b); 2008-107, s. 29.8(d); 2008-193, s. 2; 2009-444, s. 3; 2009-451, s. 15.20(h), (i); 2009-570, s. 29; 2011-145, s. 31.23(d); 2011-344, s. 2; 2011-391, s. 62; 2012-142, s. 16.5(e); 2013-225, s. 4(c); 2013-360, s. 18B.17(c).)

§ 7A-308. Miscellaneous fees and commissions.

(a)   The following miscellaneous fees and commissions shall be collected by the clerk of superior court and remitted to the State for the support of the General Court of Justice:
(1)   Foreclosure under power of sale in deed of trust or mortgage............ $300.00

If the property is sold under the power of sale, an additional amount will be charged, determined by the following formula: forty-five cents (.45) per one hundred dollars ($100.00), or major fraction thereof, of the final sale price. If the amount determined by the formula is less than ten dollars ($10.00), a minimum ten dollar ($10.00) fee will be collected. If the amount determined by the formula is more than five hundred dollars ($500.00), a maximum five hundred-dollar ($500.00) fee will be collected.

(2)   Proceeding supplemental to execution.. 30.00

(3)   Confession of judgment.. 25.00

(4)   Taking a deposition.. 10.00

(5)   Execution.. 25.00

(6)   Notice of resumption of former name.. 10.00

(7)   Taking an acknowledgment or administering an oath, or both, with or without seal, each certificate (except that oaths of office shall be administered to public officials without charge)... $2.00

(8)   Bond, taking justification or approving... 10.00

(9)   Certificate, under seal... 3.00

(10)   Exemplification of records.. 10.00

(11)   Recording or docketing (including indexing) any document
- first page... 6.00

- each additional page or fraction thereof... .25

(12)   Preparation of copies - first page (of each document copied)................. 2.00

- each additional page or fraction thereof... .25

(13)   Preparation and docketing of transcript of judgment............................
10.00

(14)   Substitution of trustee in deed of trust..
10.00

(15)   Execution of passport application - the amount allowed by federal law

(16)   Repealed by Session Laws 1989, c. 783, s. 2.

(17)   Criminal record search except if search is requested by an agency of the
State or any of its political subdivisions or by an agency of the United States or
by a petitioner in a proceeding under Article 2 of General Statutes Chapter
20................. 25.00

(18)   Filing the affirmations, acknowledgments, agreements and resulting
orders entered into under the provisions of G.S. 110-132 and G.S. 110-
133.................... 6.00

(19)   Repealed by Session Laws 1989, c. 783, s. 3.

(20)   Filing a motion to assert a right of access under G.S. 1-72.1.................
30.00

(21)   (For applicability, see Editor's note) In civil matters, all alias and pluries
summons issued and all endorsements issued on an original
summons................. $15.00.

(b)   The fees and commissions set forth in this section are not chargeable
when the service is performed as a part of the regular disposition of any action
or special proceeding or the administration of an estate. When a transaction
involves more than one of the services set forth in this section, only the greater
service fee shall be charged. The Director of the Administrative Office of the
courts shall issue guidelines pursuant to G.S. 7A-343(3) to be followed in
administering this subsection.

(b1)   The fees set forth in subdivisions (9) and (12) of subsection (a) of this
section are not chargeable when copies or certificates under seal are requested
by an attorney who has been appointed or who is under contract with the Office
of Indigent Defense Services to represent an indigent person at State expense,

if the request is made in connection with the appointed case or the contract and during the duration of the appointment or the contract.

(c)   A person who participates in a program for the collection of worthless checks under G.S. 14-107.2 must pay a fee of sixty dollars ($60.00). The fee collected under this subsection must be remitted to the State by the clerk of the court in the county in which the program is established and credited to the Collection of Worthless Checks Fund. The Collection of Worthless Checks Fund is created as a special revenue fund. Revenue in the Fund does not revert at the end of the fiscal year, and interest and other investment income earned by the Fund accrues to the Fund. The money in the Fund is subject to appropriation by the General Assembly and may be used solely for the expenses of the programs established under G.S. 14-107.2 for the collection of worthless checks, including personnel, equipment, and other costs of district attorneys' offices that are attributable to the provision of these programs. (1965, c. 310, s. 1; 1967, c. 691, ss. 32, 33; 1969, c. 1190, s. 31; 1971, c. 956, s. 2; 1973, c. 503, s. 16; c. 886; 1975, c. 829; 1981, c. 313, s. 1; 1983, c. 713, s. 18; 1985, c. 475, ss. 2, 3; c. 481, ss. 6-8; c. 511, s. 2; 1989, c. 783, ss. 2-4; c. 786, ss. 1, 3; 1997-114, s. 1; 1997-443, s. 18.22(a); 1998-23, s. 11; 1998-212, s. 16.3; 1999-237, s. 17.7; 2000-67, s. 15.3A(a); 2000-109, s. 4(e); 2001-516, s. 2; 2002-126, ss. 29A.7(a), 29A.13.1(a); 2002-135, s. 4; 2003-284, s. 36A.2; 2005-251, s. 1; 2007-323, ss. 30.8(e), (f), 30.10(c); 2008-193, s. 2; 2009-317, s. 1; 2009-451, s. 15.20(l); 2011-145, s. 31.23(e); 2011-285, s. 1; 2013-225, s. 4(d).)

§ 7A-308.1. Fees on deposits and investments.

On all funds received by the clerk by virtue or color of his office and deposited pursuant to G.S. 7A-112.1 or invested pursuant to G.S. 7A-112, one or both of the fees provided for in this section shall be assessed and collected as follows:

(1)   On all funds deposited by the clerk in an interest bearing checking account pursuant to G.S. 7A-112.1, a fee of four percent (4%) of each principal amount so deposited shall be assessed and collected, subject to the following conditions:

a.   The fee shall be collected from interest earnings only and shall not exceed the amount of the interest earnings on any principal amount so deposited, or seven hundred fifty dollars ($750.00), whichever is less;

b.   All fees collected pursuant to this subsection shall be paid to the county as court facilities fees and used as prescribed in G.S. 7A-304(a)(2);

c.   All interest earnings in excess of the prescribed fee shall be remitted to the beneficial owner or owners of any principal amount when that amount is withdrawn and distributed by the clerk; and

d.   If any principal amount is withdrawn from the checking account and invested pursuant to G.S. 7A-112, any interest in excess of the prescribed clerk's fee which is invested with the principal amount shall be included in the fund upon which the fee provided for in subdivision (2) is computed.

(2)   On all funds to be invested by the clerk pursuant to G.S. 7A-112, a fee equal to five percent (5%) of each fund shall be assessed and collected, subject to the following conditions:

a.   The fee shall be charged and deducted from each fund before the fund is invested, and only the balance shall be invested;

b.   Over the life of an account, the fees charged on the initial funds and all funds subsequently placed with the clerk for that account shall not exceed the investment earnings on the account or one thousand dollars ($1,000), whichever is less;

c.   All fees collected pursuant to this subsection shall be remitted to the State Treasurer for the support of the General Court of Justice; and

d.   Any fees charged in excess of the cumulative investment earnings on an account shall be refunded and all investment earnings in excess of the prescribed fee shall be remitted to the beneficial owner or owners when all funds in that account are finally withdrawn and distributed by the clerk. (1989, c. 783, s. 5.)

§ 7A-309. Magistrate's special fees.

The following special fees shall be collected by the magistrate and remitted to the clerk of superior court for the use of the State in support of the General Court of Justice:

(1)   Performing marriage ceremony
$20.00

(2)   Hearing petition for year's allowance to surviving spouse or child, issuing notices to commissioners, allotting the same, and making return
8.00

(3)   Taking a deposition
10.00

(4)   Proof of execution or acknowledgment of any instrument
2.00

(5)   Performing any other statutory function not incident to a civil or criminal action $
2.00.

(1965, c. 310, s. 1; 1973, c. 503, s. 17; 1983, c. 713, s. 19; 2002-126, s. 29A.10(a).)

§ 7A-310. Fees of commissioners and assessors appointed by magistrate.

Any person appointed by a magistrate as a commissioner or assessor, and who shall serve, shall be paid the sum of two dollars ($2.00), to be taxed as a part of the bill of costs of the proceeding. (1965, c. 310, s. 1.)

§ 7A-311. Uniform civil process fees.

(a)   In a civil action or special proceeding, except for actions brought under Chapter 50B of the General Statutes, the following fees and commissions shall be assessed, collected, and remitted to the county:

(1)   a.   For each item of civil process served, including summons, subpoenas, notices, motions, orders, writs and pleadings, the sum of thirty dollars ($30.00). When two or more items of civil process are served simultaneously on one party, only one thirty-dollar ($30.00) fee shall be charged.

b.   When an item of civil process is served on two or more persons or organizations, a separate service charge shall be made for each person or organization. The process fee shall be remitted to the county. This subsection shall not apply to service of summons to jurors.

c.   At least fifty percent (50%) of the fees collected pursuant to this subdivision shall be used by the county to ensure the timely service of process within the county, which may include the hiring of additional law enforcement personnel upon the recommendation of the sheriff.

(2)   For the seizure of personal property and its care after seizure, all necessary expenses, in addition to any fees for service of process.

(3)   For all sales by the sheriff of property, either real or personal, or for funds collected by the sheriff under any judgment, five percent (5%) on the first five hundred dollars ($500.00), and two and one-half percent (2 ½%) on all sums over five hundred dollars ($500.00), plus necessary expenses of sale. Whenever an execution is issued to the sheriff, and subsequently while the execution is in force and outstanding, and after the sheriff has served or attempted to serve such execution, the judgment, or any part thereof, is paid directly or indirectly to the judgment creditor, the fee herein is payable to the sheriff on the amount so paid. The judgment creditor shall be responsible for collecting and paying all execution fees on amounts paid directly to the judgment creditor.

(4)   For execution of a judgment of ejectment, all necessary expenses, in addition to any fees for service of process.

(5)   For necessary transportation of individuals to or from State institutions or another state, the same mileage and subsistence allowances as are provided for State employees.

(b)   All fees that are required to be assessed, collected, and remitted under subsection (a) of this section shall be collected in advance (except in suits in forma pauperis) except those contingent on expenses or sales prices. When the fee is not collected in advance or at the time of assessment, a lien shall exist in favor of the county on all property of the party owing the fee. If the fee remains unpaid it shall be entered as a judgment against the debtor and shall be docketed in the judgment docket in the office of the clerk of superior court.

(c)   The process fees and commissions set forth in this section are complete and exclusive and in lieu of any and all other process fees and commissions in civil actions and special proceedings. (1965, c. 310, s. 1; 1967, c. 691, s. 34; 1969, c. 1190, s. 31 1/2; 1973, c. 417, ss. 1, 2; c. 503, s. 18; c. 1139; 1979, c. 801, s. 2; 1989 (Reg. Sess., 1990), c. 1044, s. 2; 1998-212, s. 29A.12(e); 2002-126, ss. 29A.6(f), 29A.6(g); 2004-113, s. 1; 2011-145, s. 31.26(d); 2011-192, s. 7(n).)

§ 7A-312. Uniform fees for jurors; meals.

(a)   A juror in the General Court of Justice including a petit juror, or a coroner's juror, but excluding a grand juror, shall receive twelve dollars ($12.00) for the first day of service and twenty dollars ($20.00) per day afterwards, except that if any person serves as a juror for more than five days in any 24-month period, the juror shall receive forty dollars ($40.00) per day for each day of service in excess of five days. A grand juror shall receive twenty dollars ($20.00) per day. A juror required to remain overnight at the site of the trial shall be furnished adequate accommodations and subsistence. If required by the presiding judge to remain in a body during the trial of a case, meals shall be furnished the jurors during the period of sequestration. Jurors from out of the county summoned to sit on a special venire shall receive mileage at the same rate as State employees. Persons summoned as jurors shall be exempt during their period of service from paying a ferry toll required under G.S. 136-82 to travel to and from their homes and the site of that service.

(b)   Notwithstanding subsection (a) of this section, the Administrative Office of the Courts may select a judicial district to operate a pilot program in which a juror may waive payment of the per diem fees provided for in that subsection. A juror waiving the fee may designate that the fee be used for any of the following services, if such services are provided in the district: (i) client treatment and service programs associated with a drug treatment or DWI treatment court program; (ii) courthouse self-help centers; (iii) courthouse child care centers; (iv) legal aid programs operated by a nonprofit corporation operating within the district; and (v) the Crime Victims Compensation Fund. If no such services are provided within the district, then waived fees are transferred to the Crime Victims Compensation Fund. (1965, c. 310, s. 1; 1967, c. 1169; 1969, c. 1190, s. 32; 1971, c. 377, s. 26; 1973, c. 503, s. 19; 1979, c. 985; 1983, c. 881, ss. 2, 3; 1989, c. 646, s. 2; 1995, c. 324, ss. 21.1(a), (c); 2006-66, s. 14.17; 2006-187, s. 9; 2007-393, s. 16; 2012-180, s. 13.)

§ 7A-313. Uniform jail fees.

Persons who are lawfully confined in jail awaiting trial shall be liable to the county or municipality maintaining the jail in the sum of ten dollars ($10.00) for each 24 hours' confinement, or fraction thereof, except that a person so confined shall not be liable for this fee if the case or proceeding against him is dismissed, or if acquitted, or if judgment is arrested, or if probable cause is not found, or if the grand jury fails to return a true bill.

Persons who are ordered to pay jail fees pursuant to a probationary sentence shall be liable to the county or municipality maintaining the jail at the same per diem rate paid by the Division of Adult Correction of the Department of Public Safety to local jails for maintaining a prisoner, as set by the General Assembly in its appropriations acts. (1965, c. 310, s. 1; 1969, c. 1190, s. 33; 1973, c. 503, s. 20; 1975, c. 444; 1989, c. 733, s. 1; 2000-109, s. 5; 2000-140, s. 104; 2011-145, ss. 19.1(h), 31.26(e); 2011-192, s. 7(n).)

§ 7A-313.1. Fee for costs of electronic monitoring.

A county that provides the personnel, equipment, and other costs of providing electronic monitoring as a condition of an offender's bond or pretrial release may collect a fee from the offender that is the lesser of the amount of the jail fee authorized in G.S. 7A-313 or the actual cost of providing the electronic monitoring. A county may not collect a fee from an offender who is determined to be indigent and entitled to court-appointed counsel. (2011-378, s. 1.)

§ 7A-314. Uniform fees for witnesses; experts; limit on number.

(a)   A witness under subpoena, bound over, or recognized, other than a salaried State, county, or municipal law-enforcement officer, or an out-of-state witness in a criminal case, whether to testify before the court, Judicial Standards Commission, jury of view, magistrate, clerk, referee, commissioner, appraiser, or arbitrator shall be entitled to receive five dollars ($5.00) per day, or fraction thereof, during his attendance, which, except as to witnesses before the Judicial Standards Commission, must be certified to the clerk of superior court. Compensation of witnesses acting on behalf of the court or prosecutorial offices shall be paid in accordance with the rules established by the Administrative Office of the Courts. Compensation of witnesses provided under G.S. 7A-454 shall be in accordance with rules established by the Office of Indigent Defense Services.

(b)   A witness entitled to the fee set forth in subsection (a) of this section, and a law-enforcement officer who qualifies as a witness, shall be entitled to receive reimbursement for travel expenses as follows:

(1)   A witness whose residence is outside the county of appearance but within 75 miles of the place of appearance shall be entitled to receive mileage reimbursement at the rate currently authorized for State employees, for each mile necessarily traveled from his place of resident to the place of appearance and return, each day. Reimbursements to witnesses acting on behalf of the court or prosecutorial offices shall be paid in accordance with the rules established by the Administrative Office of the Courts. Reimbursements to witnesses provided under G.S. 7A-454 shall be in accordance with rules established by the Office of Indigent Defense Services.

(2)   A witness whose residence is outside the county of appearance and more than 75 miles from the place of appearance shall be entitled to receive mileage reimbursement at the rate currently authorized State employees for one round-trip from his place of residence to the place of appearance. A witness required to appear more than one day shall be entitled to receive reimbursement for actual expenses incurred for lodging and meals not to exceed the maximum currently authorized for State employees, in lieu of daily mileage. Reimbursements to witnesses acting on behalf of the court or prosecutorial offices shall be paid in accordance with the rules established by the Administrative Office of the Courts. Reimbursements to witnesses provided under G.S. 7A-454 shall be in accordance with rules established by the Office of Indigent Defense Services.

(c)   A witness who resides in a state other than North Carolina and who appears for the purpose of testifying in a criminal action and proves his attendance may be compensated at the rate allowed to State officers and employees by subdivisions (1) and (2) of G.S. 138-6(a) for one round-trip from his place of residence to the place of appearance, and five dollars ($5.00) for each day that he is required to travel and attend as a witness, upon order of the court based upon a finding that the person was a necessary witness. If such a witness is required to appear more than one day, he is also entitled to reimbursement for actual expenses incurred for lodging and meals, not to exceed the maximum currently authorized for State employees. Reimbursements to witnesses acting on behalf of the court or prosecutorial offices shall be paid in accordance with the rules established by the Administrative Office of the Courts. Reimbursements to witnesses provided under G.S. 7A-454 shall be in accordance with rules established by the Office of Indigent Defense Services.

(d)   An expert witness, other than a salaried State, county, or municipal law-enforcement officer, shall receive such compensation and allowances as the court, or the Judicial Standards Commission, in its discretion, may authorize. A law-enforcement officer who appears as an expert witness shall receive reimbursement for travel expenses only, as provided in subsection (b) of this section. Compensation of experts acting on behalf of the court or prosecutorial offices shall be paid in accordance with the rules established by the Administrative Office of the Courts. Compensation of experts provided under G.S. 7A-454 shall be in accordance with rules established by the Office of Indigent Defense Services.

(e)   If more than two witnesses are subpoenaed, bound over, or recognized, to prove a single material fact, the expense of the additional witnesses shall be borne by the party issuing or requesting the subpoena.

(f)   Repealed by Session Laws 2012-142, s. 16.3(a), effective July 1, 2012. (1965, c. 310, s. 1; 1969, c. 1190, s. 34; 1971, c. 377, s. 27; 1973, c. 503, ss. 21, 22; 1983, c. 713, s. 20; 1998-212, s. 16.25(a); 2000-144, s. 3; 2006-187, s. 5(a); 2007-323, s. 14.23; 2010-31, s. 15.7; 2011-391, s. 64; 2012-142, s. 16.3(a).)

§ 7A-314.1. Family court fees.

(a)   The Administrative Office of the Courts may charge a uniform fee of not more than fifty dollars ($50.00) per hour to persons receiving the services of a supervised visitation and exchange center through a family court program. The fees collected under this section may be used by the Director of the Administrative Office of the Courts to support the continued operation of supervised visitation and exchange centers which provide services to family court clients regarding domestic violence, substance abuse, mental illness, parental alienation, and other issues.

(b)   The Director of the Administrative Office of the Courts may establish a procedure for persons to apply for a reduction in the fee, based upon the person's ability to pay as a result of indigence, status as a victim of domestic violence, or other circumstances. (2004-110, s. 7.1; 2013-304, s. 1.)

§ 7A-315. Liability of State for witness fees in criminal cases when defendant not liable.

In a criminal action, if no prosecuting witness is designated by the court as liable for the costs, and the defendant is acquitted, or convicted and unable to pay, or a nolle prosequi is entered, or judgment is arrested, or probable cause is not found, or the grand jury fails to return a true bill, the State shall be liable for the witness fees allowed per G.S. 7A-314 and any expenses for blood tests and comparisons incurred per G.S. 8-50.1(a). (1965, c. 310, s. 1; 1979, c. 576, s. 4.)

§ 7A-316. Payment of witness fees in criminal actions.

A witness in a criminal action who is entitled to a witness fee and who proves his attendance prior to assessment of the bill of costs shall be paid by the clerk from State funds and the amount disbursed shall be assessed in the bill of costs. When the State is liable for the fee, a witness who proves his attendance not later than the last day of court in the week in which the trial was completed shall be paid by the clerk from State funds. If more than two witnesses shall be subpoenaed, bound over, or recognized, to prove a single material fact, disbursements to such additional witnesses shall be charged against the party issuing or requesting the subpoena. (1965, c. 310, s. 1; 1971, c. 377, s. 28.)

§ 7A-317. Counties and municipalities required to advance costs and fees.

(a)   Counties and municipalities required to advance pay all costs and fees due to the court at the time of filing. The clerk of superior court may consent to allow the county or municipality to pay all costs and fees within 45 days of the date of the filing of any action in lieu of paying costs and fees at the time of filing.

(b)   The clerk of superior court shall withhold all facilities fees due to be remitted to a county or municipality when the county or municipality does not pay costs and fees due to the court within 90 days of the date of filing any action. (1967, c. 691, s. 35; 2007-323, s. 30.10(d); 2008-193, ss. 1-3; 2013-225, s. 5.)

§ 7A-317.1. Disposition of fees in counties with unincorporated seats of court.

Notwithstanding any other provision of this Article, if a municipality listed in G.S. 7A-133 as an additional seat of district court is not incorporated, the arrest, facilities, and jail fees which would ordinarily accrue thereto, shall instead accrue to the county in which the unincorporated municipality is located. (1969, c. 1190, s. 34 1/2.)

§ 7A-318. Determination and disbursement of costs on and after date district court established.

(a)   On and after the date that the district court is established in a judicial district, costs in every action, proceeding or other matter pending in the General Court of Justice in that district, shall be assessed as provided in this Article, unless costs have been finally assessed according to prior law. In computing costs as provided in this section, the parties shall be given credit for any fees, costs, and commissions paid in the pending action, proceeding or other matter, before the district court was established in the district, except that no refunds are authorized.

(b)   In the administration of estates, costs shall be considered finally assessed according to prior law when they have been assessed at the time of the filing of any inventory, account, or other report. Costs at any filing on or after the date the district court is established in a judicial district shall be assessed as provided in this Article.

(c)   When the General Court of Justice fee and the facilities fee are assessed as provided in this Article and credit is given for fees, costs, and commissions paid before the district court was established in the district, the actual amount thereafter received by the clerk shall be remitted to the State for the support of the General Court of Justice.

(d)   When costs have been finally assessed according to prior law, but come into the hands of the clerk after the district court is established in the district, funds so received shall be disbursed according to prior law.

(e)   Cost funds in the hands of the clerk at the time the district court is established shall be disbursed according to prior law. (1965, c. 310, s. 1; 1967, c. 691, s. 35.)

§ 7A-319. Repealed by Session Laws 1971, c. 377, s. 32.

§ 7A-320. Costs are exclusive.

The costs set forth in this Article are complete and exclusive, and in lieu of any other costs and fees. (1983, c. 713, s. 1.)

§ 7A-321. Collection of offender fines and fees assessed by the court; collection assistance fee.

(a)   The Judicial Department may, in lieu of payment by cash or check, accept payment by credit card, charge card, or debit card for the fines, fees, and costs owed to the courts by offenders.

(b)   In attempting to collect the fines, fees, costs, and restitution owed by offenders not sentenced to supervised probation or active time, the Administrative Office of the Courts may do the following:

(1)   Assess a collection assistance fee if an amount due remains unpaid for 30 days after the time period allotted by the court. The amount of the collection assistance fee shall not exceed the average cost of collecting the debt or twenty percent (20%) of the amount past due, whichever is less.

(2)   Enter into contracts with a collection agency, agencies, or municipal or county government agencies to collect unpaid amounts owed. The Administrative Office of the Courts may provide by such contract for the collection assistance fee to be retained by the agency or agencies that collect the amounts owed.

(3)   Intercept tax refund checks under Chapter 105A of the General Statutes, the Setoff Debt Collection Act.

(c)   Repealed by Session Laws 2011-323, s. 1, effective July 1, 2011, and applicable to cases adjudicated on or after that date.

(d)   The court shall retain a collection assistance fee in the amount of ten percent (10%) of any cost or fee collected by the Department pursuant to this Article or Chapter 20 of the General Statutes and remitted to an agency of the State or any of its political subdivisions, other than a cost or fee listed in this subsection. The court shall remit the collection assistance fee to the State Treasurer for the support of the General Court of Justice.

The collection assistance fee shall not be retained from the following:

(1)   Costs and fees designated by law for remission to or use by an agency or program of the Judicial Department or for support of the General Court of Justice.

(2)   Costs and fees designated by law for remission to the General Fund.

(3)   Costs and fees designated by law for remission to the Statewide Misdemeanant Confinement Fund. (2006-187, s. 1(a); 2007-323, s. 30.9(a); 2009-451, s. 15.20(m); 2009-575, s. 14; 2011-145, s. 31.26(f1); 2011-192, ss. 7(n), 7(p); 2011-323, s. 1.)

§§ 7A-322 through 7A-339. Reserved for future codification purposes.

SUBCHAPTER VII. ADMINISTRATIVE MATTERS.

Article 29.

Administrative Office of the Courts.

§ 7A-340. Administrative Office of the Courts; establishment; officers.

There is hereby established a State office to be known as the Administrative Office of the Courts. It shall be supervised by a Director, assisted by an assistant director. (1965, c. 310, s. 1.)

§ 7A-341. Appointment and compensation of Director.

The Director shall be appointed by the Chief Justice of the Supreme Court, to serve at his pleasure. He shall receive the annual salary provided in the Current Operations Appropriations Act, payable monthly, and reimbursement for travel and subsistence expenses at the same rate as State employees generally and longevity pay at the rates and for the service designated in G.S. 7A-44(b) for a judge of the superior court. Service as Director shall be equivalent to service as a superior court judge for the purposes of entitlement to retirement pay or to retirement for disability. (1965, c. 310, s. 1; 1967, c. 691, s. 36; 1983 (Reg. Sess., 1984), c. 1034, s. 165; 1987 (Reg. Sess., 1988), c. 1100, s. 15(a).)

§ 7A-342. Appointment and compensation of assistant director and other employees.

The assistant director shall also be appointed by the Chief Justice, to serve at his pleasure. The assistant director shall receive the annual salary provided in the Current Operations Appropriations Act, payable monthly, and reimbursement for travel and subsistence expenses at the same rate as State employees generally and longevity pay at the rates and for the service designated in G.S. 7A-144(b) for a judge of the district court.

The Director may appoint such other assistant and employees as are necessary to enable him to perform the duties of his office. (1965, c. 310, s. 1; 1967, c. 691, s. 37; 1983 (Reg. Sess., 1984), c. 1034, s. 165; 1987 (Reg. Sess., 1988), c. 1100, s. 15(b).)

§ 7A-343. Duties of Director.

The Director is the Administrative Officer of the Courts, and the Director's duties include all of the following:

(1)   Collect and compile statistical data and other information on the judicial and financial operation of the courts and on the operation of other offices directly related to and serving the courts.

(2)   Determine the state of the dockets and evaluate the practices and procedures of the courts, and make recommendations concerning the number of judges, district attorneys, and magistrates required for the efficient administration of justice.

(3)   Prescribe uniform administrative and business methods, systems, forms and records to be used in the offices of the clerks of superior court.

(3a)   Maintain and staff as necessary an Internal Audit Division of the Judicial Department and the Administrative Office of the Courts that:

a.   Evaluates and discloses potential weaknesses in the effectiveness of internal controls in the court system for the purpose of safeguarding public funds and assets and minimizing incidences of fraud, waste, and abuse.

b.   Examines and analyzes the design and effectiveness of administrative and procedural operations.

c.   Ensures overall compliance with federal and State laws, internal and external regulations, rules and procedures, and other applicable requirements.

d.   Inspects and reviews the effectiveness and efficiency of processes and proceedings conducted by judicial officers.

e.   Collaborates with other divisions to guide, direct, and support court officials in efforts to conform to both recommended and required compliance standards.

f.   Executes routine audits of the Judicial Department's systems and controls, including, but not limited to:

1.   Accounting systems and controls.

2.   Administrative systems and controls.

3.   Electronic data processing systems and controls.

(4)   Prepare and submit budget estimates of State appropriations necessary for the maintenance and operation of the Judicial Department, and authorize expenditures from funds appropriated for these purposes.

(5)   Investigate, make recommendations concerning, and assist in the securing of adequate physical accommodations for the General Court of Justice.

(6)   Procure, distribute, exchange, transfer, and assign such equipment, books, forms and supplies as are to be acquired with State funds for the General Court of Justice.

(7)   Make recommendations for the improvement of the operations of the Judicial Department.

(8)   Prepare and submit an annual report on the work of the Judicial Department to the Chief Justice, and transmit a copy to each member of the General Assembly. The annual report shall include the activities of each North Carolina Business Court site, including the number of new, closed, and pending cases, the average age of pending cases, and the annual expenditures for the prior fiscal year.

(9)   Assist the Chief Justice in performing his duties relating to the transfer of district court judges for temporary or specialized duty.

(9a)   Establish and operate systems and services that provide for electronic filing in the court system and further provide electronic transaction processing and access to court information systems pursuant to G.S. 7A-343.2.

(9b)   Enter into contracts with one or more private vendors to provide for the payment of fines, fees, and costs due to the court by credit, charge, or debit cards; such contracts may provide for the assessment of a convenience or transaction fee by the vendor to cover the costs of providing this service.

(9c)   Prescribe policies and procedures for the appointment and payment of foreign language interpreters. These policies and procedures shall be applied uniformly throughout the General Court of Justice. After consultation with the Joint Legislative Commission on Governmental Operations, the Director may also convert contractual foreign language interpreter positions to permanent State positions when the Director determines that it is more cost-effective to do so.

(9d)   Analyze the use of contractual positions in the Judicial Department and, after consultation with the Joint Legislative Commission on Governmental Operations, convert contractual positions to permanent State positions when the Director determines it is in the best interests of the Judicial Department to do so.

(9e)   Prescribe policies and procedures for the appointment and payment of deaf and hearing-impaired interpreters, in accordance with G.S. 8B-8(a), for those cases specified in G.S. 8B-8(b) and (c). These policies and procedures shall be applied uniformly throughout the General Court of Justice. After consultation with the Joint Legislative Commission on Governmental Operations, the Director may also convert contractual hearing-impaired interpreter positions to permanent State positions when the Director determines that it is more cost-effective to do so.

104

(9f)   Prescribe policies and procedures for the payment of those experts acting on behalf of the court or prosecutorial offices, as provided for in G.S. 7A-314(d).

(10)   Perform such additional duties and exercise such additional powers as may be prescribed by statute or assigned by the Chief Justice.

(11)   Prescribe policies and procedures for the assignment and compensation of magistrates performing temporary duty outside their county of residence during an emergency, as provided for in G.S. 7A-146(9).

(12)   Issue photographic identification cards to appropriate Judicial Department employees and officials authorizing those employees and officials to travel to and from, enter, and work in court and court-related locations for the conduct or support of essential court operations in preparation for, during, or in the aftermath of emergency situations, including, but not limited to, catastrophic conditions. Notwithstanding any other provision of the law, and notwithstanding any emergency restrictions on travel or closures that may have been issued due to the emergency situations, an identification card issued pursuant to this subdivision shall be honored by all State and local law enforcement, emergency and health officers, and other authorities to permit the person to whom the card was issued to travel to and from court and court-related locations and otherwise carry out the purposes authorized by this subdivision. An identification card issued pursuant to this subdivision shall set forth its effective date and the full name, position, and employing unit of the person to whom the card is issued, with a provision, signed by the person, stating that the person is credentialed solely for the purposes stated in this subdivision and that the card shall not be used for any other purpose.

(13)   Prescribe policies and procedures and establish and operate systems for the exchange of criminal and civil information from and to the Judicial Department and local, State, and federal governments and the Eastern Band of Cherokee Indians.

(14)   Transfer equipment and supply funds to the appropriate programs and between programs as the equipment priorities and supply consumptions occur during the operating year.

(15)   Notwithstanding the provisions of G.S. 138-6(a)(1), elect to establish a per-mile reimbursement rate for transportation by privately owned vehicles at a rate less than the business standard mileage rate set by the Internal Revenue

105

Service. (1965, c. 310, s. 1; 1967, c. 1049, s. 5; 1973, c. 47, s. 2; 1999-237, s. 17.15(a); 2006-187, ss. 1(b), 2(b), 5(b); 2007-393, s. 11; 2009-516, s. 3; 2010-31, s. 15.12.; 2011-411, s. 2(a); 2012-142, s. 16.3(b).)

§ 7A-343.1. Distribution of copies of the appellate division reports.

The Administrative Officer of the Courts shall, at the State's expense distribute such number of copies of the appellate division reports to federal, State departments and agencies, and to educational institutions of instruction, as follows:

Governor, Office of the
1

Lieutenant Governor, Office of the
1

Secretary of State, Department of the
2

State Auditor, Department of the
1

Treasurer, Department of the State
1

Superintendent of Public Instruction
1

Office of the Attorney General
11

State Bureau of Investigation
1

Agriculture and Consumer Services, Department of
1

Labor, Department of
1

Insurance, Department of
1

Budget Bureau, Department of Administration
1

Property Control, Department of Administration
1

State Planning, Department of Administration
1

Environment and Natural Resources, Department of
1

Revenue, Department of
1

Health and Human Services, Department of
1

Juvenile Justice, Division of
1

Commission for the Blind
1

Transportation, Department of
1

Motor Vehicles, Division of
1

Utilities Commission
8

Industrial Commission
11

State Human Resources Commission
1

Office of State Human Resources
1

Office of Administrative Hearings
2

Community Colleges, Department of
38

Department of Commerce
1

Commission of Correction
1

Parole Commission
1

Archives and History, Division of
1

Public Safety, Department of
2

Cultural Resources, Department of
3

Legislative Building Library
2

Justices of the Supreme Court
1 ea.

Judges of the Court of Appeals
1 ea.

Judges of the Superior Court
1 ea.

Clerks of the Superior Court
1 ea.

District Attorneys
1 ea.

Emergency and Special Judges of the Superior Court
1 ea.

Supreme Court Library
AS MANY AS

REQUESTED

Appellate Division Reporter
1

University of North Carolina, Chapel Hill
71

University of North Carolina, Charlotte
1

University of North Carolina, Greensboro
1

University of North Carolina, Asheville
1

North Carolina State University, Raleigh
1

Appalachian State University
1

East Carolina University
1

Fayetteville State University
1

North Carolina Central University
17

Western Carolina University
1

Duke University
17

Davidson College
2

Wake Forest University
25

Lenoir Rhyne College
1

Elon College
1

Campbell University
25

Federal, Out-of-State and Foreign Secretary of State
1

Secretary of Defense
1

Secretary of Health, Education and Welfare
1

Secretary of Housing and Urban Development
1

Secretary of Transportation
1

Attorney General
1

Department of Justice
1

Internal Revenue Service
1

Veterans' Administration
1

Library of Congress
5

Federal Judges resident in North Carolina
1 ea.

Marshal of the United States Supreme Court
1

Federal District Attorneys resident in North Carolina
1 ea.

Federal Clerks of Court resident in North Carolina
1 ea.

Supreme Court Library exchange list
1

Cherokee Supreme Court, Eastern Band of

Cherokee Indians
1

Each justice of the Supreme Court and judge of the Court of Appeals shall receive for private use, one complete and up-to-date set of the appellate division reports. The copies of reports furnished each justice or judge as set out in the table above may be retained personally to enable the justice or judge to keep up-to-date the personal set of reports. (1973, c. 476, s. 84; 1977, c. 379, s. 2; c.

771, s. 4; 1979, c. 899, s. 1; 1979, 2nd Sess., c. 1278; 1985 (Reg. Sess., 1986), c. 1022, s. 2; 1987, c. 877, s. 1; 1989, c. 727, s. 218(1); 1993, c. 257, s. 19; 1995, c. 166, s. 1; c. 509, s. 4; 1997-261, s. 109; 1997-443, s. 11A.7; 1998-202, s. 4(a); 2000-137, s. 4(b); 2001-280, s. 1; 2011-145, ss. 19.1(g), 19.1(dd); 2011-401, s. 3.1; 2013-382, s. 9.1(c).)

§ 7A-343.2. Court Information Technology Fund.

(a)   Fund. - The Court Information Technology Fund is established within the Judicial Department as a special revenue fund. Interest and other investment income earned by the Fund accrues to it. The Fund consists of the following revenues:

(1)   All monies collected by the Director pursuant to G.S. 7A-109(d) and G.S. 7A-49.5.

(2)   State judicial facilities fees credited to the Fund under G.S. 7A-304 through G.S. 7A-307.

(b)   Use. - Money in the Fund derived from State judicial facilities fees must be used to upgrade, maintain, and operate the judicial and county courthouse phone systems. All other monies in the Fund must be used to supplement funds otherwise available to the Judicial Department for court information technology and office automation needs.
(c)   Report. - The Director must report by August 1 and February 1 of each year to the Joint Legislative Commission on Governmental Operations, the Chairs of the Senate and House Appropriations Committees, and the Chairs of the Senate and House Appropriations Subcommittees on Justice and Public Safety. The report must include the following:

(1)   Amounts credited in the preceding six months to the Fund.

(2)   Amounts expended in the preceding six months from the Fund and the purposes of the expenditures.

(3)   Proposed expenditures of the monies in the Fund. (1999-237, s. 17.15(b); 2000-67, s. 15.1; 2006-187, s. 2(d); 2008-107, s. 29.8(e); 2009-570, s. 2.; 2012-142, s. 16.5(a))

§ 7A-343.3. Appellate Courts Printing and Computer Operations Fund.

The Appellate Courts Printing and Computer Operations Fund is established within the Judicial Department as a nonreverting, interest-bearing special revenue account. Accordingly, interest and other investment income earned by the Fund shall be credited to it. All moneys collected through charges to litigants for the reproduction of appellate records and briefs under G.S. 7A-11 and G.S. 7A-20(b) shall be remitted to the State Treasurer and held in this Fund. Moneys in the Fund shall be used to support the print shop operations of the Supreme Court and the Court of Appeals, including personnel, maintenance, and capital costs. The Judicial Department may create and maintain receipt-supported positions for these purposes but shall report to the Chairs of the Senate and House of Representatives Appropriations Subcommittees on Justice and Public Safety prior to creating such new positions.

The Judicial Department shall report to the Chairs of the Senate and House of Representatives Appropriations Subcommittees on Justice and Public Safety by January 1 of each year on all receipts and expenditures of the Fund. (2002-126, s. 14.12.)

§ 7A-343.4. Internal audit standards; report and work papers.

(a)   Internal audits shall comply with current Standards for the Professional Practice of Internal Auditing issued by the Institute for Internal Auditors and, when appropriate, Government Auditing Standards issued by the Comptroller General of the United States.

(b)   Except as otherwise provided in this section, the Internal Audit Division shall maintain all audit reports, examinations, investigations, surveys, drafts, work papers, and all other documents prepared by the internal auditors in accordance with the North Carolina Court System's Rules of Recordkeeping and Records Retention and Disposition Schedule (the Rules). Except as provided in this section, or upon an order issued in Wake County Superior Court upon 10 days' notice and hearing finding that access is necessary to a proper administration of justice, audit work papers, drafts, and all audit documents other than the final audit report are available only to the Internal Audit Division, the Director, the Chief Financial Officer, Legal Services, and other persons in the internal auditor's discretion for the limited purpose of ensuring the accuracy and reliability of the final audit report. Pertinent work papers and other supportive material related to issued audit reports may be, at the discretion of the internal auditor and unless otherwise prohibited by law, made available for inspection by duly authorized representatives of the State and federal government who desire access to and inspection of such records in connection with some matter officially before them, including criminal investigations.

(c)   Where the professional guidelines, government standards, and the Rules fail to specify or are in conflict, the Rules shall govern. (2009-516, s. 5.)

§ 7A-343.5. Definitions.

The following definitions apply in this Article:

(1)   "Accounting system" means the total structure of records and procedures which discover, record, classify, and report information on the financial position and operating results of the Judicial Department, or a segment of the Judicial Department, or any of its funds, balanced account groups, and organizational components.

(2)   "Internal auditing" means an independent, objective assurance and consulting activity designed to add value to and improve an organization's operations. Internal auditing helps an organization accomplish its objectives by using a systematic, disciplined approach to evaluate and improve the effectiveness of risk management, controls, and governance processes. The types of audits the internal auditors may provide include, but are not limited to:
a.   Efficiency or economy audits to evaluate areas at risk and require improvements to promote operating effectiveness and efficiency, mitigate the risk of liability, and realize economies.

b.   Financial audits to determine whether financial operations are properly functioning.

c.   Compliance audits or reviews to assess compliance with laws and regulations.

d.   Internal control audits to assess the controls related to financial transactions and reporting.

e.   Case file and procedural audits to ensure efficiency, effectiveness, and compliance.

114

f.   Performance and management audits entail an objective and systematic examination of evidence to provide an independent assessment of the performance and management of a program against objective criteria as well as assessments that provide a prospective focus or that synthesize information on best practices.

g.   Investigative or fraud audits to make an independent assessment of allegations of fraud, misuse, or process manipulation or alleged violations of federal, State, or local laws. (2009-516, s. 6.)

§ 7A-344: Repealed by Session Laws 2000-144, s. 4.

§ 7A-345. Duties of assistant director.

The assistant director is the administrative assistant to the Chief Justice, and his duties include the following:

(1)   Assist the Chief Justice in performing his duties relating to the assignment of superior court judges;

(2)   Assist the Supreme Court in preparing calendars of superior court trial sessions; and

(3)   Performing such additional functions as may be assigned by the Chief Justice or the Director of the Administrative Office. (1965, c. 310, s. 1; 1969, c. 1013, s. 4.)

§ 7A-346. Information to be furnished to Administrative Officer.

All judges, district attorneys, public defenders, magistrates, clerks of superior court and other officers or employees of the courts and of offices directly related to and serving the courts shall on request furnish to the Administrative Officer information and statistical data relative to the work of the courts and of such offices and relative to the receipt and expenditure of public moneys for the operation thereof. (1965, c. 310, s. 1; 1967, c. 1049, s. 5; 1969, c. 1013, ss. 4, 5; 1973, c. 47, s. 2.)

§ 7A-346.1: Repealed by Session Laws 2000-67, s. 15(b).

§ 7A-346.2. Various reports to General Assembly.

(a)   The Administrative Office of the Courts and the Office of Indigent Defense Services shall report by March 1 of each year to the Chairs of the House of Representatives and Senate Appropriations Committees, to the Chairs of the House of Representatives Subcommittee on Justice and Public Safety, and to the Chairs of the Senate Appropriations Committee on Justice and Public Safety on contracts entered into with local governments for the provision of the services of assistant district attorneys, assistant public defenders, judicial secretaries, and employees in the office of the Clerk of Superior Court. The report shall include the number of applications made to the Administrative Office of the Courts or the Office of Indigent Defense Services for these contracts, the number of contracts entered for provision of these positions, and the dollar amounts of each contract.

(b)   The Administrative Office of the Courts shall report by April 1 of each odd-numbered year to the Chairs of the Senate and House Appropriations Committees and the Chairs of the Senate and House Appropriations Subcommittees on Justice and Public Safety on the economic viability of the worthless check collection programs established by district attorneys pursuant to G.S. 14-107.2, including an assessment of whether any adjustments need to be made to ensure that the programs, on a statewide basis, are self-supporting. (1999-237, s. 17.7(c); 2000-67, ss. 15.3A(b), 15.4(h); 2001-61, s. 2; 2001-424, s. 22.11(g); 2003-377, s. 4.)

§ 7A-346.3. (Contingent effective date - see editor's note) Impaired driving integrated data system report.

The information compiled by G.S. 7A-109.2 shall be maintained in an Administrative Office of the Courts database. By March 1, the Administrative Office of the Courts shall provide an annual report of the previous calendar year to the Joint Legislative Commission on Governmental Operations and the Joint Legislative Oversight Committee on Justice and Public Safety. The annual report shall show the types of dispositions for the entire State by county, by judge, by prosecutor, and by defense attorney. This report shall also include the amount of fines, costs, and fees ordered at the disposition of the charge, the amount of any subsequent reduction, amount collected, and the amount still

116

owed, and compliance with sanctions of community service, jail, substance abuse assessment, treatment, and education. The Administrative Office of the Courts shall facilitate public access to the information collected under this section by posting this information on the court's Internet page in a manner accessible to the public and shall make reports of any information collected under this section available to the public upon request and without charge. (2006-253, s. 20.2; 2011-291, s. 2.1.)

§ 7A-347. Assistants for administrative and victim and witness services.

Assistant for administrative and victim and witness services positions are established under the district attorneys' offices. Each prosecutorial district is allocated at least one assistant for administrative and victim and witness services to be employed by the district attorney. The Administrative Office of the Courts shall allocate additional assistants to prosecutorial districts on the basis of need and within available appropriations. Each district attorney may also use any volunteer or other personnel to assist the assistant. The assistant is responsible for coordinating efforts of the law-enforcement and judicial systems to assure that each victim and witness is provided fair treatment under Article 45 of Chapter 15A, Fair Treatment for Victims and Witnesses and shall also provide administrative and legal support to the district attorney's office. (1985 (Reg. Sess., 1986), c. 998, s. 2; 1997-443, s. 18.7(c).)

§ 7A-348. Training and supervision of assistants for administrative and victim and witness services.

Pursuant to the provisions of G.S. 7A-413, the Conference of District Attorneys shall:

(1)   Assist in establishing uniform statewide training for assistants for administrative and victim and witness services; and

(2)   Assist in the implementation and supervision of this program. (1985 (Reg. Sess., 1986), c. 998, s. 2; 1997-443, s. 18.7(d); 2001-424, s. 22.6(a).)

§ 7A-349. Criminal history record check; denial of employment, contract, or volunteer opportunity.

117

The Judicial Department may deny employment, a contract, or a volunteer opportunity to any person who refuses to consent to a criminal history check authorized under G.S. 114-19.19 and may dismiss a current employee, terminate a contractor, or terminate a volunteer relationship if that employee, contractor, or volunteer refuses to consent to a criminal history record check authorized under G.S. 114-19.19. (2006-187, s. 3(b).)

§§ 7A-350 through 7A-354. Reserved for future codification purposes.

Article 29A.

Trial Court Administrators.

§ 7A-355. Trial court administrators.

The following districts or sets of districts as defined in G.S. 7A-41.1(a) shall have trial court administrators: Set of districts 10A, 10B, 10C, 10D; District 22 and District 28, and such other districts or sets of districts as may be designated by the Administrative Office of the Courts. (1979, c. 1072, s. 10; 1987 (Reg. Sess., 1988), c. 1037, s. 27.)

§ 7A-356. Duties.

The duties of each trial court administrator shall be to assist in managing civil dockets, to improve jury utilization and to perform such duties as may be assigned by the senior resident superior court judge of his district or set of districts as defined in G.S. 7A-41.1(a) or by other judges designated by that senior resident superior court judge. (1979, c. 1072, s. 10; 1987 (Reg. Sess., 1988), c. 1037, s. 28.)

§§ 7A-357 through 7A-374. Reserved for future codification purposes.

Article 30.

Judicial Standards Commission.

118

§ 7A-374.1. Purpose.

The purpose of this Article is to provide for the investigation and resolution of inquiries concerning the qualification or conduct of any judge or justice of the General Court of Justice. The procedure for discipline of any judge or justice of the General Court of Justice shall be in accordance with this Article. Nothing in this Article shall affect the impeachment of judges under the North Carolina Constitution, Article IV, Sections 4 and 17. (2006-187, s. 11.)

§ 7A-374.2. Definitions.

Unless the context clearly requires otherwise, the definitions in this section shall apply throughout this Article:

(1)   "Censure" means a finding by the Supreme Court, based upon a written recommendation by the Commission, that a judge has willfully engaged in misconduct prejudicial to the administration of justice that brings the judicial office into disrepute, but which does not warrant the suspension of the judge from the judge's judicial duties or the removal of the judge from judicial office. A censure may require that the judge follow a corrective course of action. Unless otherwise ordered by the Supreme Court, the judge shall personally appear in the Supreme Court to receive a censure.

(2)   "Commission" means the North Carolina Judicial Standards Commission.

(3)   "Incapacity" means any physical, mental, or emotional condition that seriously interferes with the ability of a judge to perform the duties of judicial office.

(4)   "Investigation" means the gathering of information with respect to alleged misconduct or disability.

(5)   "Judge" means any justice or judge of the General Court of Justice of North Carolina, including any retired justice or judge who is recalled for service as an emergency judge of any division of the General Court of Justice.

(6)   "Letter of caution" means a written action of the Commission that cautions a judge not to engage in certain conduct that violates the Code of Judicial Conduct as adopted by the Supreme Court.

119

(7) "Public reprimand" means a finding by the Supreme Court, based upon a written recommendation by the Commission that a judge has violated the Code of Judicial Conduct and has engaged in conduct prejudicial to the administration of justice, but that misconduct is minor. A public reprimand may require that the judge follow a corrective course of action.

(8) "Remove" or "removal" means a finding by the Supreme Court, based upon a written recommendation by the Commission, that a judge should be relieved of all duties of the judge's office and disqualified from holding further judicial office.

(9) "Suspend" or "suspension" means a finding by the Supreme Court, based upon a written recommendation by the Commission, that a judge should be relieved of the duties of the judge's office for a period of time, and upon conditions, including those regarding treatment and compensation, as may be specified by the Supreme Court. (2006-187, s. 11; 2013-404, s. 1.)

§ 7A-375. Judicial Standards Commission.

(a) The Judicial Standards Commission shall consist of the following residents of North Carolina: one Court of Appeals judge, two superior court judges, and two district court judges, each appointed by the Chief Justice of the Supreme Court; four members of the State Bar who have actively practiced in the courts of the State for at least 10 years, elected by the State Bar Council; and four citizens who are not judges, active or retired, nor members of the State Bar, two appointed by the Governor, and two appointed by the General Assembly in accordance with G.S. 120-121, one upon recommendation of the President Pro Tempore of the Senate and one upon recommendation of the Speaker of the House of Representatives. The Court of Appeals judge shall act as chair of the Commission.

(b) The Court of Appeals judge shall serve at the pleasure of the Chief Justice. Terms of other Commission members shall be for six years. No member who has served a full six-year term is eligible for reappointment. If a member ceases to have the qualifications required for the member's appointment, that person ceases to be a member. Vacancies of members, other than those appointed by the General Assembly, are filled in the same manner as the original appointment, for the remainder of the term. Vacancies of members appointed by the General Assembly are filled as provided under G.S. 120-122. Members who are not judges are entitled to per diem and all members

120

are entitled to reimbursement for travel and subsistence expenses at the rate applicable to members of State boards and commissions generally, for each day engaged in official business.

(c)　　If a member of the Commission who is a judge becomes disabled, or becomes a respondent before the Commission, the Chief Justice shall appoint an alternate member to serve during the period of disability or disqualification. The alternate member shall be from the same division of the General Court of Justice as the judge whose place the alternate member takes. If a member of the Commission who is not a judge becomes disabled, the Governor, if he appointed the disabled member, shall appoint, or the State Bar Council, if it elected the disabled member, shall elect, an alternate member to serve during the period of disability. If a member of the Commission who is not a judge and who was appointed by the General Assembly becomes disabled, an alternate member shall be appointed to serve during the period of disability in the same manner as if there were a vacancy to be filled under G.S. 120-122. In a particular case, if a member becomes disqualified, or is successfully challenged for cause, the member's seat for that case shall be filled by an alternate member selected as provided in this subsection.

(d)　　A member may serve after expiration of the member's term only to participate until the conclusion of a disciplinary proceeding begun before expiration of the member's term. Such participation shall not prevent the successor from taking office, but the successor may not participate in the proceeding for which the predecessor's term was extended. This subsection shall apply also to any judicial member whose membership on the Commission is automatically terminated by retirement or resignation from judicial office, or expiration of the term of judicial office.

(e)　　Members of the Commission and its employees are immune from civil suit for all conduct undertaken in the course of their official duties.

(f)　　The chair of the Commission may employ, if funds are appropriated for that purpose, an executive director, Commission counsel, investigator, and any support staff as may be necessary to assist the Commission in carrying out its duties. With the approval of the Chief Justice, for specific cases, the chair also may employ special counsel or call upon the Attorney General to furnish counsel. In addition, with the approval of the Chief Justice, for specific cases, the chair or executive director also may call upon the Director of the State Bureau of Investigation to furnish an investigator who shall serve under the supervision of the executive director. While performing duties for the

Commission, the executive director, counsel, and investigator have authority throughout the State to serve subpoenas or other process issued by the Commission in the same manner and with the same effect as an officer authorized to serve process of the General Court of Justice.

(g)   The Commission may adopt, and may amend from time to time, its own rules of procedure for the performance of the duties and responsibilities prescribed by this Article, subject to the approval of the Supreme Court. (1971, c. 590, s. 1; 1973, c. 50; 1975, c. 956, s. 13; 1997-72, s. 1; 2006-187, s. 11.)

§ 7A-376. Grounds for discipline by Commission; public reprimand, censure, suspension, or removal by the Supreme Court.

(a)   The Commission, upon a determination that any judge has engaged in conduct that violates the North Carolina Code of Judicial Conduct as adopted by the Supreme Court but that is not of such a nature as would warrant a recommendation of public reprimand, censure, suspension, or removal, may issue to the judge a private letter of caution.

(b)   Upon recommendation of the Commission, the Supreme Court may issue a public reprimand, censure, suspend, or remove any judge for willful misconduct in office, willful and persistent failure to perform the judge's duties, habitual intemperance, conviction of a crime involving moral turpitude, or conduct prejudicial to the administration of justice that brings the judicial office into disrepute. A judge who is suspended for any of the foregoing reasons shall receive no compensation during the period of that suspension. A judge who is removed for any of the foregoing reasons shall receive no retirement compensation and is disqualified from holding further judicial office.

(c)   Upon recommendation of the Commission, the Supreme Court may suspend, for a period of time the Supreme Court deems necessary, any judge for temporary physical or mental incapacity interfering with the performance of the judge's duties, and may remove any judge for physical or mental incapacity interfering with the performance of the judge's duties which is, or is likely to become, permanent. A judge who is suspended for temporary incapacity shall continue to receive compensation during the period of the suspension. A judge removed for mental or physical incapacity is entitled to retirement compensation if the judge has accumulated the years of creditable service required for incapacity or disability retirement under any provision of State law, but he shall

122

not sit as an emergency justice or judge. (1971, c. 590, s. 1; 1979, c. 486, s. 2; 2006-187, s. 11; 2013-404, s. 2.)

§ 7A-377. Procedures.

(a)   Any citizen of the State may file a written complaint with the Commission concerning the qualifications or conduct of any justice or judge of the General Court of Justice, and thereupon the Commission shall make such investigation as it deems necessary. The Commission may also make an investigation on its own motion. The Commission may issue process to compel the attendance of witnesses and the production of evidence, to administer oaths, and to punish for contempt. No justice or judge shall be recommended for public reprimand, censure, suspension, or removal unless he has been given a hearing affording due process of law.

(a1)   Unless otherwise waived by the justice or judge involved, all papers filed with and proceedings before the Commission, including any investigation that the Commission may make, are confidential, and no person shall disclose information obtained from Commission proceedings or papers filed with or by the Commission, except as provided herein. Those papers are not subject to disclosure under Chapter 132 of the General Statutes.

(a2)   Information submitted to the Commission or its staff, and testimony given in any proceeding before the Commission, shall be absolutely privileged, and no civil action predicated upon that information or testimony may be instituted against any complainant, witness, or his or her counsel.

(a3)   If, after an investigation is completed, the Commission concludes that a letter of caution is appropriate, it shall issue to the judge a letter of caution in lieu of any further proceeding in the matter. The issuance of a letter of caution is confidential in accordance with subsection (a1) of this section.

(a4)   Repealed by Session Laws 2013-404, s. 3, effective August 23, 2013.

(a5)   If, after an investigation is completed, the Commission concludes that disciplinary proceedings should be instituted, the notice and statement of charges filed by the Commission, along with the answer and all other pleadings, remain confidential. Disciplinary hearings ordered by the Commission are confidential, and recommendations of the Commission to the Supreme Court, along with the record filed in support of such recommendations are confidential.

123

Testimony and other evidence presented to the Commission is privileged in any action for defamation. At least five members of the Commission must concur in any recommendation to issue a public reprimand, censure, suspend, or remove any judge. A respondent who is recommended for public reprimand, censure, suspension, or removal is entitled to a copy of the proposed record to be filed with the Supreme Court, and if the respondent has objections to it, to have the record settled by the Commission's chair. The respondent is also entitled to present a brief and to argue the respondent's case, in person and through counsel, to the Supreme Court. A majority of the members of the Supreme Court voting must concur in any order of public reprimand, censure, suspension, or removal. The Supreme Court may approve the recommendation, remand for further proceedings, or reject the recommendation. A justice of the Supreme Court or a member of the Commission who is a judge is disqualified from acting in any case in which he is a respondent.

(a6)   Upon issuance of a public reprimand, censure, suspension, or removal by the Supreme Court, the notice and statement of charges filed by the Commission along with the answer and all other pleadings, and recommendations of the Commission to the Supreme Court along with the record filed in support of such recommendations, are no longer confidential.

(b)   Repealed by Session Laws 2006-187, s. 11, effective January 1, 2007.

(c)   The Commission may issue advisory opinions to judges, in accordance with rules and procedures adopted by the Commission.

(d)   The Commission has the same power as a trial court of the General Court of Justice to punish for contempt, or for refusal to obey lawful orders or process issued by the Commission. (1971, c. 590, s. 1; 1973, c. 808; 1989 (Reg. Sess., 1990), c. 995, s. 2; 1997-72, s. 2; 2006-187, s. 11; 2013-404, s. 3.)

§ 7A-378: Repealed by Session Laws 2013-404, s. 4, effective August 23, 2013.

§§ 7A-379 through 7A-399. Reserved for future codification purposes.

Article 31.

Judicial Council.

§§ 7A-400 through 7A-408. Repealed by Session Laws 1983, c.774, s. 1.

Article 31A.

State Judicial Council.

§ 7A-409. Composition of State Judicial Council.

(a)   The State Judicial Council shall consist of 18 members as follows:

(1)   The Chief Justice, who chairs the Council;

(2)   The Chief Judge of the Court of Appeals;

(3)   A district attorney chosen by the Conference of District Attorneys;

(4)   A public defender chosen by the public defenders;

(5)   A superior court judge chosen by the Conference of Superior Court Judges;

(6)   A district court judge chosen by the Conference of District Court Judges;

(7)   A clerk of superior court chosen by the Association of Clerks of Superior Court of North Carolina;

(8)   A magistrate appointed by the North Carolina Magistrates' Association;

(9)   An attorney appointed by the Council of the State Bar;

(10)   One attorney and one nonattorney appointed by the Chief Justice;

(11)   One nonattorney and one attorney appointed by the Governor;

(12)   One nonattorney and one attorney appointed by the General Assembly upon the recommendation of the Speaker of the House of Representatives;

(13)   One nonattorney and one attorney appointed by the General Assembly upon the recommendation of the President Pro Tempore of the Senate; and

(14)   One member appointed by the Commission on Indigent Defense Services.

(b)   The Chief Justice and the Chief Judge shall be members of the State Judicial Council during their terms in those judicial offices. The terms of the other members selected initially for the State Judicial Council shall be as follows:

(1)   One year. - The district court judge, the attorney appointed upon the recommendation of the President Pro Tempore of the Senate, and the attorney appointed upon the recommendation of the Speaker of the House of Representatives.

(2)   Two years. - The district attorney, the magistrate, the nonattorney appointed by the Governor, and the nonattorney appointed by the Chief Justice.

(3)   Three years. - The public defender, the attorney appointed by the Council of the State Bar, the nonattorney appointed upon the recommendation of the President Pro Tempore of the Senate, and the nonattorney appointed upon the recommendation of the Speaker of the House of Representatives.

(4)   Four years. - The superior court judge, the clerk of superior court, the attorney appointed by the Governor, the attorney appointed by the Chief Justice, and the member appointed by the Commission on Indigent Defense Services.

After these initial terms, the members of the State Judicial Council shall serve terms of four years. All terms of members shall begin on January 1 and end on December 31. No member may serve more than two consecutive full terms. Any vacancy on the Council shall be filled by a person appointed by the official or entity who appointed the person vacating the position.

(c)   If an official or entity is authorized to appoint more than one member of the State Judicial Council, the members appointed by that official or entity must reside in different judicial districts.

(d)   No incumbent member of the General Assembly or incumbent judicial official, other than the ones specifically identified by office in subsection (a) of this section, may serve on the State Judicial Council.

(e)   The appointing authorities shall confer with each other and attempt to arrange their appointments so that the members of the State Judicial Council fairly represent each area of the State, both genders, and each major racial group. (1999-390, s. 1; 2001-96, s. 1.)

§ 7A-409.1. Duties of the State Judicial Council.

(a)   The State Judicial Council shall:

(1)   Study the judicial system and report periodically to the Chief Justice on its findings;

(2)   Advise the Chief Justice on priorities for funding;

(3)   Review and advise the Chief Justice on the budget prepared by the Director of the Administrative Office of the Courts for submission to the General Assembly;

(4)   Study and recommend to the General Assembly the salaries of justices and judges;

(5)   Recommend to the General Assembly changes in the expense allowances, benefits, and other compensation for judicial officials;

(6)   Recommend the creation of judgeships; and

(7)   Advise or assist the Chief Justice, as requested, on any other matter concerning the operation of the courts.

(b)   The State Judicial Council, with the assistance of the Director of the Administrative Office of the Courts, shall recommend to the Chief Justice performance standards for all courts and all judicial officials and shall recommend procedures for periodic evaluation of the court system and individual judicial officials and employees. If these standards are implemented by the Chief Justice, the Director of the Administrative Office of the Courts shall inform each judicial official of the standards being used to evaluate that official's performance. If implemented, the evaluation of each judge shall include assessments from other judges, litigants, jurors, and attorneys, as well as a self-evaluation by the judge. Summaries of the evaluations of justices and judges shall be made available to the public, in a manner to be determined by the Council, but the data collected in producing the evaluations shall not be a public record.

127

(c)   The State Judicial Council shall study and recommend guidelines for the assignment and management of cases, including the identification of different kinds of cases for different kinds of resolution. If the Chief Justice decides to implement these guidelines, the guidelines may provide that, except for good cause, each civil case subject to assignment to a trial judge should be directed first to an appropriate form of alternative dispute resolution. The guidelines may also provide for posttrial alternative dispute resolution before or as part of an appeal. The guidelines should not require absolute uniformity from district to district and should allow case management personnel within each district the flexibility to direct cases to the most appropriate means of resolution in that district.

(d)   The State Judicial Council shall monitor the use of alternative dispute resolution throughout the court system and, with the assistance of the Director of the Administrative Office of the Courts and the Dispute Resolution Commission, evaluate the effectiveness of those programs.

(e)   The State Judicial Council may recommend changes in the boundaries of the judicial districts or divisions.

(f)   The State Judicial Council shall monitor the administration of justice and assess the effectiveness of the Judicial Branch in serving the public and to advise the Chief Justice and the General Assembly on changes needed to assist the General Court of Justice in better fulfilling its mission.

(g)   The State Judicial Council shall report to the General Assembly and the Chief Justice no later than December 31, 2009, and no later than December 31 of every third year, regarding the implementation of S.L. 2006-184 and shall include in its report the statistics regarding inquiries and any recommendations for changes. The House of Representatives and the Senate shall refer the report of the State Judicial Council to the Joint Legislative Oversight Committee on Justice and Public Safety and such other committees as the Speaker of the House of Representatives or the President Pro Tempore of the Senate shall deem appropriate, for their review. (1999-390, s. 1; 2006-184, s. 10; 2010-171, s. 5; 2011-291, s. 2.2.)

§ 7A-409.2. Compensation of the State Judicial Council.

Members of the State Judicial Council who are not officers or employees of the State shall receive compensation and reimbursement for travel and subsistence expenses at the rates specified in G.S. 138-5. Members of the State Judicial Council who are officers or employees of the State shall receive reimbursement for travel and subsistence expenses at the rate set out in G.S. 138-6. (1999-390, s. 1.)

Article 31B.

Declaration of Vacancy, Suspension of Salary.

§ 7A-410. Vacancy exists on disbarment.

When a judge of the district court, judge of the superior court, judge of the Court of Appeals, justice of the Supreme Court, or a district attorney is no longer authorized to practice law in the courts of this State, the Governor shall declare the office vacant. Prior to making such declaration, the Governor shall notify the justice, judge, or district attorney at least 10 days in advance of taking such action and shall afford the justice, judge, or district attorney the opportunity to be heard on the matter. For purposes of this Article, the term "no longer authorized to practice law" means that the person has been disbarred or suspended and all appeals under G.S. 84-28 have been exhausted. (2007-104, s. 1.)

§ 7A-410.1. Suspension of salary.

When a justice, judge, or district attorney has been disbarred or suspended from the practice of law under G.S. 84-28 but the office has not been declared vacant under G.S. 7A-410, the salary of the justice, judge, or district attorney is suspended immediately. If the order of disbarment or suspension is reversed on appeal, the salary shall be paid retroactively from the date the salary was suspended. (2007-104, s. 1.)

SUBCHAPTER VIII. CONFERENCE OF DISTRICT ATTORNEYS.

Article 32.

Conference of District Attorneys.

§ 7A-411. Establishment and purpose.

There is created the Conference of District Attorneys of North Carolina, of which every district attorney in North Carolina is a member. The purpose of the Conference is to assist in improving the administration of justice in North Carolina by coordinating the prosecution efforts of the various district attorneys, by assisting them in the administration of their offices, and by exercising the powers and performing the duties provided for in this Article. (1983, c. 761, s. 152.)

§ 7A-412. Annual meetings; organization; election of officers.

(a)   Annual Meetings. - The Conference shall meet annually at a time and place selected by the President of the Conference.

(b)   Election of Officers. - Officers of the Conference are a President, a President-elect, a Vice-president, and other officers from among its membership that the Conference may designate in its bylaws. Officers are elected for one-year terms at the annual Conference, and take office on July 1 immediately following their election.

(c)   Executive Committee. - The Executive Committee of the Conference consists of the President, the President-elect, the Vice-president, and four other members of the Conference. One of these four members shall be the immediate past president if there is one and if he continues to be a member.

(d)   Organization and Functioning; Bylaws. - The bylaws may provide for the organization and functioning of the Conference, including the powers and duties of its officers and committees. The bylaws shall state the number of members required to constitute a quorum at any meeting of the Conference or the Executive Committee. The bylaws shall set out the procedure for amending the bylaws.

(e)   Calling Meetings; Duty to Attend. - The President or the Executive Committee may call a meeting of the Conference upon 10 days' notice to the members, except upon written waiver of notice signed by at least three-fourths of the members. A member should attend each meeting of the Conference and the Executive Committee of which he is given notice. Members are entitled to reimbursement for travel and subsistence expenses at the rate applicable to State employees. (1983, c. 761, s. 152.)

§ 7A-413. Powers of Conference.

(a)   The Conference may:

(1)   Cooperate with citizens and other public and private agencies to promote the effective administration of criminal justice.

(2)   Assist prosecutors in the effective prosecution and trial of criminal offenses, and develop an advisory trial manual.

(3)   Develop advisory manuals to assist prosecutors in the organization and administration of their offices, case management, calendaring, case tracking, filing, and office procedures.

(4)   Cooperate with the Administrative Office of the Courts and the School of Government at the University of North Carolina at Chapel Hill concerning education and training programs for prosecutors and staff.

(b)   The Conference may not adopt rules pursuant to Chapter 150B of the General Statutes. (1983, c. 761, s. 152; 1987, c. 827, s. 1; 2006-264, s. 29(b).)

§ 7A-414. Executive Secretary; clerical support.

The Conference may employ an executive secretary and any necessary supporting staff to assist it in carrying out its duties. (1983, c. 761, s. 152.)

Articles 33 to 35.

§§ 7A-415 through 7A-449. Reserved for future codification purposes.

SUBCHAPTER IX. REPRESENTATION OF INDIGENT PERSONS.

Article 36.

Entitlement of Indigent Persons Generally.

§ 7A-450. Indigency; definition; entitlement; determination; change of status.

(a)   An indigent person is a person who is financially unable to secure legal representation and to provide all other necessary expenses of representation in an action or proceeding enumerated in this Subchapter. An interpreter is a necessary expense as defined in Chapter 8B of the General Statutes for a deaf person who is entitled to counsel under this subsection.

(b)   Whenever a person, under the standards and procedures set out in this Subchapter, is determined to be an indigent person entitled to counsel, it is the responsibility of the State to provide him with counsel and the other necessary expenses of representation. The professional relationship of counsel so provided to the indigent person he represents is the same as if counsel had been privately retained by the indigent person.

(b1)   An indigent person indicted for murder may not be tried where the State is seeking the death penalty without an assistant counsel being appointed in a timely manner. If the indigent person is represented by the public defender's office, the requirement of an assistant counsel may be satisfied by the assignment to the case of an additional attorney from the public defender's staff.

(c)   The question of indigency may be determined or redetermined by the court at any stage of the action or proceeding at which an indigent is entitled to representation.

(d)   If, at any stage in the action or proceeding, a person previously determined to be indigent becomes financially able to secure legal representation and provide other necessary expenses of representation, he must inform the counsel appointed by the court to represent him of that fact. In such a case, that information is not included in the attorney client privilege, and counsel must promptly inform the court of that information. (1969, c. 1013, s. 1; 1981, c. 409, s. 2; c. 937, s. 3; 1985, c. 698, s. 22(a); 2000-144, s. 5.)

§ 7A-450.1. Responsibility for payment by certain fiduciaries.

It is the intent of the General Assembly that, whenever possible, if an attorney or guardian ad litem is appointed pursuant to G.S. 7A-451 for a person who is less than 18 years old or who is at least 18 years old but remains dependent on and domiciled with a parent or guardian, the parent, guardian, or any trustee in possession of funds or property for the benefit of the person, shall reimburse the State for the attorney or guardian ad litem fees, pursuant to the procedures established in G.S. 7A-450.2 and G.S. 7A-450.3. This section shall not apply in any case in which the person for whom an attorney or guardian ad litem is appointed prevails. (1983, c. 726, s. 1; 1991 (Reg. Sess., 1992), c. 1030, s. 2.)

§ 7A-450.2. Determination of fiduciaries at indigency determination; summons; service of process.

At the same time as a person who is less than 18 years old or who is at least 18 years old but remains dependent on and domiciled with a parent or guardian is determined to be indigent, and has an attorney or guardian ad litem appointed pursuant to G.S. 7A-451, the court shall determine the identity and address of the parent, guardian or any trustee in possession of funds or property for the benefit of the person. The court shall issue a summons to the parent, guardian or trustee to be present at the dispositional hearing or the sentencing hearing or other appropriate hearing and to be a party to these hearings for the purpose of being determined responsible for reimbursing the State for the person's attorney or guardian ad litem fees, or to show cause why he should not be held responsible.

Both the issuance of the summons and the service of process shall be pursuant to G.S. 1A-1, Rule 4. (1983, c. 726, s. 1.)

§ 7A-450.3. Determination of responsibility at hearing.

At the dispositional, sentencing or other hearing of the person who is less than 18 years old or who is at least 18 years old but remains dependent on and domiciled with a parent or guardian, the court shall make a determination whether the parent, guardian or trustee should be held responsible for reimbursing the State for the person's attorney or guardian ad litem fees. This determination shall include the financial situation of the parent, guardian or trustee, the relationship of responsibility the parent, guardian or trustee bears to the person and any showings by the parent, guardian or trustee that the person is emancipated or not dependent. The test of the party's financial ability to pay is the test applied to appointment of an attorney in cases of indigency. Any provision of any deed, trust or other writing, which, if enforced, would defeat the intent or purpose of this section is contrary to the public policy of this State and is void insofar as it may apply to prohibit reimbursement to the State.

If the court determines that the parent, guardian or trustee is responsible for reimbursing the State for the attorney or guardian ad litem fees, the court shall so order. If the party does not comply with the order at the time of disposition, the court shall file a judgment against him for the amount due the State. (1983, c. 726, s. 1; 2005-254, s. 3.)

§ 7A-450.4. Exemptions.

General Statutes 7A-450.1, 7A-450.2 and 7A-450.3 do not authorize the court to require the Department of Health and Human Services or any county Department of Social Services to reimburse the State for fees. (1983, c. 726, s. 1; 1997-443, s. 11A.118(a).)

§ 7A-451. Scope of entitlement.

(a)   An indigent person is entitled to services of counsel in the following actions and proceedings:

(1)   Any case in which imprisonment, or a fine of five hundred dollars ($500.00), or more, is likely to be adjudged;

(2)   A hearing on a petition for a writ of habeas corpus under Chapter 17 of the General Statutes;

(3)   A motion for appropriate relief under Chapter 15A of the General Statutes if the defendant has been convicted of a felony, has been fined five hundred dollars ($500.00) or more, or has been sentenced to a term of imprisonment;

(4)   A hearing for revocation of probation;

(5)   A hearing in which extradition to another state is sought;

(6)   A proceeding for an inpatient involuntary commitment to a facility under Part 7 of Article 5 of Chapter 122C of the General Statutes, or a proceeding for commitment under Part 8 of Article 5 of Chapter 122C of the General Statutes.

(7)   In any case of execution against the person under Chapter 1, Article 28 of the General Statutes, and in any civil arrest and bail proceeding under Chapter 1, Article 34, of the General Statutes;

(8)   In the case of a juvenile, a hearing as a result of which commitment to an institution or transfer to the superior court for trial on a felony charge is possible;

(9)   A hearing for revocation of parole at which the right to counsel is provided in accordance with the provisions of Chapter 148, Article 4, of the General Statutes;

(10)   Repealed by Session Laws 2003, c. 13, s. 2(a), effective April 17, 2003, and applicable to all petitions for sterilization pending and orders authorizing sterilization that have not been executed as of April 17, 2003.

(11)   A proceeding for the provision of protective services according to Chapter 108A, Article 6 of the General Statutes;

(12)   In the case of a juvenile alleged to be abused, neglected, or dependent under Subchapter I of Chapter 7B of the General Statutes;

(13)   A proceeding to find a person incompetent under Subchapter I of Chapter 35A, of the General Statutes;

(14)   A proceeding to terminate parental rights where a guardian ad litem is appointed pursuant to G.S. 7B-1101;

(15)   An action brought pursuant to Article 11 of Chapter 7B of the General Statutes to terminate an indigent person's parental rights.

(16)   A proceeding involving consent for an abortion on an unemancipated minor pursuant to Article 1A, Part 2 of Chapter 90 of the General Statutes. G.S. 7A-450.1, 7A-450.2, and 7A-450.3 shall not apply to this proceeding.

(17)   A proceeding involving limitation on freedom of movement or access pursuant to G.S. 130A-475 or G.S. 130A-145.

(18)   A proceeding involving placement into satellite monitoring under Part 5 of Article 27A of Chapter 14 of the General Statutes.

(b)   In each of the actions and proceedings enumerated in subsection (a) of this section, entitlement to the services of counsel begins as soon as feasible after the indigent is taken into custody or service is made upon him of the charge, petition, notice or other initiating process. Entitlement continues through any critical stage of the action or proceeding, including, if applicable:

(1)   An in-custody interrogation;

(2)   A pretrial identification procedure which occurs after formal charges have been preferred and at which the presence of the indigent is required;

(3)   A hearing for the reduction of bail, or to fix bail if bail has been earlier denied;

(4)   A probable cause hearing;

(5)   Trial and sentencing;

(6)   Review of any judgment or decree pursuant to G.S. 7A-27, 7A-30(1), 7A-30(2), and Subchapter XIV of Chapter 15A of the General Statutes;

(7)   In a capital case in which a defendant is under a sentence of death, subject to rules adopted by the Office of Indigent Defense Services, review of any judgment or decree rendered on direct appeal by the Supreme Court of North Carolina pursuant to the certiorari jurisdiction of the United States Supreme Court; and

(8)   In a noncapital case, subject to rules adopted by the Office of Indigent Defense Services, review of any judgment or decree rendered on direct appeal by a court of the North Carolina Appellate Division pursuant to the certiorari jurisdiction of the United States Supreme Court, when the judgment or decree:

a.   Decides an important question of federal law in a way that conflicts with relevant decisions of the United States Supreme Court, a federal Court of Appeals, or the court of last resort of another state;

b.   Decides an important question of federal law that has not been, but should be, settled by the United States Supreme Court; or

c.   Decides a question of federal law in the indigent's favor and the judgment or decree is challenged by opposing counsel through an attempt to invoke the certiorari jurisdiction of the United States Supreme Court.

(c)   In any capital case, an indigent defendant who is under a sentence of death and desires counsel may apply to the Office of Indigent Defense Services for the appointment of counsel to represent the defendant in preparing, filing, and litigating a motion for appropriate relief. The application for the appointment of such postconviction counsel may be made prior to completion of review on direct appeal and shall be made no later than 10 days from the latest of the following:

(1)   The mandate has been issued by the Supreme Court of North Carolina on direct appeal pursuant to N.C.R. App. P. 32(b) and the time for filing a petition for writ of certiorari to the United States Supreme Court has expired without a petition being filed;

(2)   The United States Supreme Court denied a timely petition for writ of certiorari of the decision on direct appeal by the Supreme Court of North Carolina; or

(3)   The United States Supreme Court granted the defendant's or the State's timely petition for writ of certiorari of the decision on direct appeal by the Supreme Court of North Carolina, but subsequently left the defendant's death sentence undisturbed.

(c1)   Upon application, supported by the defendant's affidavit, the Office of Indigent Defense Services shall determine whether the defendant was previously adjudicated indigent for purposes of trial or direct appeal. If the defendant was previously adjudicated indigent, the defendant shall be presumed indigent for purposes of this subsection, and the Office of Indigent Defense Services shall appoint two counsel to represent the defendant. If the defendant was not previously adjudicated indigent, the Office of Indigent Defense Services shall request that the superior court in the district where the defendant was indicted determine whether the defendant is indigent. If the court finds that the defendant is indigent, the Office of Indigent Defense Services shall then appoint two counsel to represent the defendant.

(c2)   The defendant does not have a right to be present at the time of appointment of counsel, and the appointment need not be made in open court.

(d)   The appointment of counsel as provided in subsection (c) of this section and the procedure for compensation shall comply with rules adopted by the Office of Indigent Defense Services.

(e)   No counsel appointed pursuant to subsection (c) of this section shall have previously represented the defendant at trial or on direct appeal in the case for which the appointment is made unless the defendant expressly requests continued representation and understandingly waives future allegations of ineffective assistance of counsel.

(e1)   When the Supreme Court of North Carolina files an opinion affirming or reversing the judgment of the trial court in a case in which the defendant was sentenced to death, or files an opinion or decision with regard to such a defendant's postconviction petition for relief from a sentence of death, or when any federal court files or issues an opinion or decision in such circumstances, the Division of Adult Correction of the Department of Public Safety shall, on the day the opinion or decision is filed or issued, permit counsel for the defendant to visit the defendant at the institution at which the defendant is confined. The visit shall be permitted during regular business hours for not less than one hour, unless a visit outside regular business hours is agreed to by both the institution's administrator and counsel for the defendant. This section shall not be construed to abridge the adequate and reasonable opportunity for attorneys to consult with clients sentenced to death generally and shall not be construed to mandate an attorney visit during an emergency at the institution at which a defendant is confined.

(f)   A guardian ad litem shall be appointed to represent the best interest of an underage party seeking judicial authorization to marry pursuant to G.S. 51-2A. The appointment and duties of the guardian ad litem shall be governed by G.S. 51-2A. The procedure for compensation of the guardian ad litem shall comply with rules adopted by the Office of Indigent Defense Services. (1969, c. 1013, s. 1; 1973, c. 151, ss. 1, 3; c. 616; c. 726, s. 4; c. 1116, s. 1; c. 1125; c. 1320; c. 1378, s. 2; 1977, c. 711, ss. 7, 8; c. 725, s. 2; 1979, 2nd Sess., c. 1206, s. 3; 1981, c. 966, s. 4; 1983, c. 638, s. 23; c. 864, s. 4; 1985, c. 509, s. 1; c. 589, s. 3; 1987, c. 550, s. 16; 1995, c. 462, s. 3; 1995 (Reg. Sess., 1996), c. 719, s. 7; 1998-202, s. 13(a); 2000-144, s. 6; 2001-62, s. 14; 2002-179, s. 16; 2003-13, s. 2(a); 2005-250, s. 2; 2007-323, s. 14.19(a); 2009-91, s. 1; 2009-387, ss. 3, 5; 2011-145, s. 19.1(h).)

§ 7A-451.1. Counsel fees for outpatient involuntary commitment proceedings.

The State shall pay counsel fees for persons appointed pursuant to G.S. 122C-267(d). (1983, c. 638, s. 24; c. 864, s. 4; 1985, c. 589, s. 4; 1991, c. 761, s. 3.)

§ 7A-452. Source of counsel; fees; appellate records.

(a)   Upon the court's determination that a person is indigent and entitled to counsel under this Article, counsel shall be appointed in accordance with rules adopted by the Office of Indigent Defense Services. In noncapital cases, the court shall assign counsel pursuant to rules adopted by the Office of Indigent Defense Services. In capital cases, the Office of Indigent Defense Services or designee of the Office of Indigent Defense Services shall assign counsel; at least one member of each capital defense team, where practicable, shall be a member of the bar in that division. In the courts of those counties which have a public defender, however, the public defender may tentatively assign himself or an assistant public defender to represent an indigent person, subject to subsequent determination of entitlement to counsel by the court and approval by the court in noncapital cases and by the Office of Indigent Defense Services in capital cases.

(b)   Fees of assigned counsel and salaries and other operating expenses of the offices of the public defenders shall be borne by the State.

(c)   (1)   The clerk of superior court is authorized to make a determination of indigency and entitlement to counsel, as authorized by this Article. The word "court," as it is used in this Article and in any rules pursuant to this Article, includes the clerk of superior court.

(2)   A judge of superior or district court having authority to determine entitlement to counsel in a particular case may give directions to the clerk with regard to the determination of entitlement to counsel in that case; may, if he finds it appropriate, change or modify the determination made by the clerk; and may set aside a finding of waiver of counsel made by the clerk.

(d)   Unless a public defender or assistant public defender is appointed to serve, standby counsel appointed under G.S. 15A-1243 shall receive reasonable compensation to be paid by the State.

(e)   In cases in which an indigent person has entered notice of appeal and appellate counsel has been appointed by the Office of Indigent Defense Services, the clerk of superior court shall make a copy of the complete trial division file in the case, make a copy of documentary exhibits upon request, and furnish those files and any requested documentary exhibits to the appointed attorney. (1969, c. 1013, s. 1; 1971, c. 377, s. 32; 1973, c. 1286, s. 8; 1977, c. 711, s. 9; 1987 (Reg. Sess., 1988), c. 1037, s. 29; 2000-144, s. 7; 2005-148, s. 1.)

§ 7A-453. Duty of custodian of a possibly indigent person; determination of indigency.

(a)   In counties designated by the Office of Indigent Defense Services, the authority having custody of a person who is without counsel for more than 48 hours after being taken into custody shall so inform the designee of the Office of Indigent Defense Services. The designee of the Office of Indigent Defense Services shall make a preliminary determination as to the person's entitlement to his services, and proceed accordingly. The court shall make the final determination.

(b)   In counties that have not been designated by the Office of Indigent Defense Services, the authority having custody of a person who is without counsel for more than 48 hours after being taken into custody shall so inform the clerk of superior court.

(c)   In any county, if a defendant, upon being taken into custody, states that he is indigent and desires counsel, the authority having custody shall immediately inform the designee of the Office of Indigent Defense Services or the clerk of superior court, as the case may be, who shall take action as provided in this Article.

(d)   The duties imposed by this section upon authorities having custody of persons who may be indigent are in addition to the duties imposed upon arresting officers under G.S. 15-47. (1969, c. 1013, s. 1; 1973, c. 1286, s. 8; 1987 (Reg. Sess., 1988), c. 1037, s. 30; 2000-144, s. 8.)

§ 7A-454. Supporting services.

Fees for the services of an expert witness or other witnesses, paid in accordance with G.S. 7A-314, including travel expenses, lodging, and other appearance expenses, for an indigent person and other necessary expenses of counsel shall be paid by the State in accordance with rules adopted by the Office of Indigent Defense Services. (1969, c. 1013, s. 1; 2000-144, s. 9; 2011-145, s. 31.23C(b); 2011-391, s. 64.)

§ 7A-455. Partial indigency; liens; acquittals.

(a)	If, in the opinion of the court, an indigent person is financially able to pay a portion, but not all, of the value of the legal services rendered for that person by assigned counsel, the public defender, or the appellate defender, and other necessary expenses of representation, the court shall order the partially indigent person to pay such portion to the clerk of superior court for transmission to the State treasury.

(b)	In all cases the court shall direct that a judgment be entered in the office of the clerk of superior court for the money value of services rendered by assigned counsel, the public defender, or the appellate defender, plus any sums allowed for other necessary expenses of representing the indigent person, including any fees and expenses that may have been allowed prior to final determination of the action to assigned counsel pursuant to G.S. 7A-458, which shall constitute a lien as prescribed by the general law of the State applicable to judgments. Any reimbursement to the State as provided in subsection (a) of this section or any funds collected by reason of such judgment shall be deposited in the State treasury and credited against the judgment. The value of services shall be determined in accordance with rules adopted by the Office of Indigent Defense Services. The money value of services rendered by the public defender and the appellate defender shall be based upon the factors normally involved in fixing the fees of private attorneys, such as the nature of the case, the time, effort, and responsibility involved, and the fee usually charged in similar cases. A district court judge shall direct entry of judgment for actions or proceedings finally determined in the district court and a superior court judge shall direct entry of judgment for actions or proceedings originating in, heard on appeal in, or appealed from the superior court. Even if the trial, appeal, hearing, or other proceeding is never held, preparation therefor is nevertheless compensable.

(b1)	In every case in which the State is entitled to a lien pursuant to this section, the public defender shall at the time of sentencing or other conclusion of the proceedings petition the court to enter judgment for the value of the legal services rendered by the public defender, and the appellate defender shall upon completion of the appeal petition or request the trial court to enter judgment for the value of the legal services rendered by the appellate defender.

(c)	No order for partial payment under subsection (a) of this section and no judgment under subsection (b) of this section shall be entered unless the indigent person is convicted. If the indigent person is convicted, the order or judgment shall become effective and the judgment shall be docketed and indexed pursuant to G.S. 1-233 et seq., in the amount then owing, upon the later of (i) the date upon which the conviction becomes final if the indigent

141

person is not ordered, as a condition of probation, to pay the State of North Carolina for the costs of his representation in the case or (ii) the date upon which the indigent person's probation is terminated, is revoked, or expires if the indigent person is so ordered. No order for partial payment under subsection (a) of this section and no judgment under subsection (b) of this section shall be entered for the value of legal services rendered to perfect an appeal to the Appellate Division or in postconviction proceedings, if all of the matters that the person raised in the proceeding are vacated, reversed, or remanded for a new trial or resentencing.

(d)   In all cases in which the entry of a judgment is authorized under G.S. 7A-450.1 through G.S. 7A-450.4 or under this section, the attorney, guardian ad litem, public defender, or appellate defender who rendered the services or incurred the expenses for which the judgment is to be entered shall make reasonable efforts to obtain the social security number, if any, of each person against whom judgment is to be entered. This number, a certification that the person has no social security number, or a certification that the social security number cannot be obtained with reasonable efforts shall be included in each fee application submitted by an assigned attorney, guardian ad litem, public defender, or appellate defender, and no order for payment entered upon an application which does not include the required social security number or certification shall be valid to authorize payment to the applicant from the Indigent Persons' Attorney Fee Fund. Each judgment docketed against any person under this section or under G.S. 7A-450.3 shall include the social security number, if any, of the judgment debtor. (1969, c. 1013, s. 1; 1983, c. 135, s. 2; 1983 (Reg. Sess., 1984), c. 1109, s. 12; 1985, c. 474, s. 9; 1989 (Reg. Sess., 1990), c. 946, ss. 5, 6; 1991, c. 761, s. 4; 1991 (Reg. Sess., 1992), c. 900, s. 116(a); 2000-144, s. 10; 2005-254, s. 1; 2013-41, s. 1.)

§ 7A-455.1. Appointment fee in criminal cases.

(a)   In every criminal case in which counsel is appointed at the trial level, the judge shall order the defendant to pay to the clerk of court an appointment fee of sixty dollars ($60.00). No fee shall be due unless the person is convicted.

(b)   The mandatory sixty-dollar ($60.00) fee may not be remitted or revoked by the court and shall be added to any amounts the court determines to be owed for the value of legal services rendered to the defendant and shall be collected in the same manner as attorneys' fees are collected for such representation.

142

(c)   Repealed by Session Laws 2005-250 s. 3, effective August 4, 2005.

(d)   Inability, failure, or refusal to pay the appointment fee shall not be grounds for denying appointment of counsel, for withdrawal of counsel, or for contempt.

(e)   The appointment fee required by this section shall be assessed only once for each attorney appointment, regardless of the number of cases to which the attorney was assigned. An additional appointment fee shall not be assessed if the charges for which an attorney was appointed were reassigned to a different attorney.

(f)   Of each appointment fee collected under this section, the sum of fifty-five dollars ($55.00) shall be credited to the Indigent Persons' Attorney Fee Fund and the sum of five dollars ($5.00) shall be credited to the Court Information Technology Fund under G.S. 7A-343.2. These fees shall not revert.

(g)   The Office of Indigent Defense Services shall adopt rules and develop forms to govern implementation of this section. (2002-126, s. 29A.9(a); 2003-284, s. 13.11; 2005-250, s. 3; 2009-451, s. 15.17l(a); 2010-31, s. 15.11(a); 2012-142, s. 16.5(h).)

§ 7A-456. False statements; penalty.

(a)   A false material statement made by a person under oath or affirmation in regard to the question of his indigency constitutes a Class I felony.

(b)   A judicial official making the determination of indigency shall notify the person of the provisions of subsection (a) of this section.

(c)   Repealed by Session Laws 1987 (Reg. Sess., 1988), c. 1100, s. 11.1. (1969, c. 1013, s. 1; 1987 (Reg. Sess., 1988), c. 1086, s. 113(c); c. 1100, s. 11.1; 1993 (Reg. Sess., 1994), c. 767, s. 19.)

§ 7A-457. Waiver of counsel; pleas of guilty.

(a)   An indigent person who has been informed of his right to be represented by counsel at any in-court proceeding, may, in writing, waive the right to in-court representation by counsel in accordance with rules adopted by the Office of

143

Indigent Defense Services. Any waiver of counsel shall be effective only if the court finds of record that at the time of waiver the indigent person acted with full awareness of his rights and of the consequences of the waiver. In making such a finding, the court shall consider, among other things, such matters as the person's age, education, familiarity with the English language, mental condition, and the complexity of the crime charged.

(b)   If an indigent person waives counsel as provided in subsection (a), and pleads guilty to any offense, the court shall inform him of the nature of the offense and the possible consequences of his plea, and as a condition of accepting the plea of guilty the court shall examine the person and shall ascertain that the plea was freely, understandably and voluntarily made, without undue influence, compulsion or duress, and without promise of leniency.

(c)   An indigent person who has been informed of his right to be represented by counsel at any out-of-court proceeding, may, either orally or in writing, waive the right to out-of-court representation by counsel. (1969, c. 1013, s. 1; 1971, c. 1243; 1973, c. 151, s. 3; 2000-144, s. 11.)

§ 7A-458. Counsel fees.

The fee to which an attorney who represents an indigent person is entitled shall be fixed in accordance with rules adopted by the Office of Indigent Defense Services. Fees shall be based on the factors normally considered in fixing attorneys' fees, such as the nature of the case, and the time, effort and responsibility involved. Fees shall not be set or ordered at rates higher than those established by the rules adopted under this section without the approval of the Office of Indigent Defense Services. Even if the trial, appeal, hearing or other proceeding is never held, preparation therefor is nevertheless compensable and, in capital cases and other extraordinary cases pending in superior court, a fee for services rendered and payment for expenses incurred may be allowed pending final determination of the case. (1969, c. 1013, s. 1; 1987 (Reg. Sess., 1988), c. 1086, s. 113(b); 1991 (Reg. Sess., 1992), c. 900, s. 116(b); 2000-144, s. 12; 2005-276, s. 14.13.)

§ 7A-459: Repealed by Session Laws 2000-144, s. 13, as amended by Session Laws 2001-424, s. 22.11(c).

§§ 7A-460 through 7A-464: Reserved for future codification purposes.

Article 37.

The Public Defender.

§§ 7A-465 through 7A-467: Repealed by Session Laws 2000-144, s. 13, as amended by Session Laws 2001-424, s. 22.11(c).

§ 7A-468: Repealed by Session Laws 1987 (Regular Session, 1988), c. 1056, s. 13.

§§ 7A-469 through 7A-471: Repealed by Session Laws 2000-144, s. 13, as amended by Session Laws 2001-424, s. 22.11(c), effective July 1, 2001.

§ 7A-472. Reserved for future codification purposes.

§ 7A-473. Reserved for future codification purposes.

§ 7A-474. Reserved for future codification purposes.

Article 37A.

Access to Civil Justice Act.

§ 7A-474.1. Legislative findings and purpose.

The General Assembly of North Carolina declares it to be its purpose to provide access to legal representation for indigent persons in certain kinds of civil matters. The General Assembly finds that such representation can best be provided in an efficient, effective, and economic manner through the established legal services programs in this State. (1989, c. 795, s. 25; 2001-424, s. 22.14(e); 2007-323, s. 30.8(g).)

§ 7A-474.2. Definitions.

The following definitions shall apply throughout this Article, unless the context otherwise requires:

(1)   "Eligible client" means a resident of North Carolina financially eligible for representation under the Legal Services Corporation Act, regulations, and interpretations adopted thereunder (45 C.F.R. § 1611, and subsequent revisions), or a person entitled to State benefits or services pursuant to G.S. 14-43.11(d).

(1a)   "Established legal services programs" means the following not-for-profit corporations using State funds to serve the counties listed: Legal Services of the Southern Piedmont, serving Cabarrus, Gaston, Mecklenburg, Stanly, and Union Counties; Pisgah Legal Services, serving Buncombe, Henderson, Madison, Polk, Rutherford, and Transylvania Counties; and Legal Aid of North Carolina, a statewide program; or any successor entity or entities of the named organizations, or, should any of the named organizations dissolve, the entity or entities providing substantially the same services in substantially the same service area.

(2)   "Legal assistance" means the provision of any legal services, as defined by Chapter 84 of the General Statutes, consistent with this Article. Provided, that all legal services provided hereunder shall be performed consistently with the Rules of Professional Conduct promulgated by the North Carolina State Bar. Provided, further, that no funds appropriated under this Article shall be used for lobbying to influence the passage or defeat of any legislation before any municipal, county, state, or national legislative body.

(3)   Repealed by Session Laws 2001-424, s. 22.14(f), effective January 1, 2002.

(4)   Recodified as subdivision (1a). (1989, c. 795, s. 25; 2001-424, s. 22.14(f); 2007-323, s. 30.8(h); 2007-547, s. 9; 2008-194, s. 3(a).)

§ 7A-474.3. Eligible activities and limitations.

(a)   Eligible Activities. Funds appropriated under this Article shall be used only for the following purposes:

(1)   To provide legal assistance to eligible clients;

(2)   To provide education to eligible clients regarding their rights and duties under the law;

(3)   To involve the private bar in the representation of eligible clients pursuant to this Article.

(b)   Eligible Cases. Legal assistance shall be provided to eligible clients under this Article only in the following types of cases:

(1)   Family violence or spouse abuse;

(2)   Assistance for the disabled in obtaining federal Social Security benefits;

(2a)   Assistance for eligible clients in obtaining benefits or assistance under any federal law or program providing benefits or assistance for human trafficking victims.

(3)   Representation of eligible farmers faced with the potential of farm foreclosure;

(4)   Representation of eligible clients over the age of 60 regarding the following matters:

a.   Wills and estates;

b.   Safe and sanitary housing;

c.   Pensions and retirement rights;

d.   Social Security and Medicare rights;

e.   Access to health care;

f.   Food and nutrition; and

g.   Transportation.

(5)   Representation of eligible clients designed to enable them to obtain the necessary skills and means to obtain meaningful employment at a decent wage and reduce the public welfare rolls; and

(6)   Representation of eligible clients under the age of 21 or eligible families with legal problems affecting persons under the age of 21 regarding the following matters:

a.   Financial support and custody of children;

b.   Child care;

c.   Child abuse or neglect;
d.   Safe and sanitary housing;

e.   Food and nutrition; and

f.   Access to health care.

(7)   Legal assistance to consumers in cases involving predatory mortgage lending, mortgage broker and loan services abuses, foreclosure defense, and other legal issues that relate to helping consumers avoid foreclosure and home loss.

(c)   Limitations. No funds appropriated under this Article shall be used for any of the following purposes:

(1)   To provide legal assistance with respect to any proceeding or litigation which seeks to procure a nontherapeutic abortion or to compel any individual or institution to perform an abortion, or assist in the performance of an abortion, or provide facilities for the performance of an abortion;

(2)   To provide legal assistance with respect to any criminal proceeding;

(3)   To provide legal assistance to any agricultural employee or migrant farmworker employed in North Carolina with regard to the terms of the worker's employment, including conditions relating to housing;

(4)   To provide legal assistance to any prisoner within the Division of Adult Correction of the Department of Public Safety with regard to the terms of that person's incarceration; or

(5)   To provide legal assistance to persons with mental handicaps residing in State institutions with regard to the terms and conditions of the treatment or services provided to them by the State. (1989, c. 795, s. 25; 1997-506, s. 29; 2007-547, s. 10; 2008-107, s. 14.9; 2011-145, s. 19.1(h); 2012-83, s. 15.)

§ 7A-474.4. Funds.

Funds to provide representation pursuant to this Article shall be provided to the North Carolina State Bar for provision of direct services by and support of the established legal services programs. The North Carolina State Bar shall allocate these funds directly to each of the established legal services programs based upon the eligible client population in each area, with Pisgah Legal Services receiving the allocation for Buncombe, Henderson, Madison, Polk, Rutherford, and Transylvania Counties; and Legal Services of Southern Piedmont receiving half of the allocation for Cabarrus, Gaston, Mecklenburg, Stanly, and Union Counties. The North Carolina State Bar shall not use any of these funds for its administrative costs. (1989, c. 795, s. 25; 2001-424, s. 22.14(g); 2007-323, s. 30.8(i); 2008-194, s. 3(b).)

§ 7A-474.5. Records and reports.

The established legal services programs shall keep appropriate records and make periodic reports, as requested, to the North Carolina State Bar. (1989, c. 795, s. 25; 2001-424, s. 22.14(h); 2007-323, s. 30.8(j).)

§§ 7A-474.6 through 7A-474.15: Reserved for future codification purposes.

Article 37B.

Domestic Violence Victim Assistance Act.

§ 7A-474.16. Legislative findings and purpose.

The General Assembly of North Carolina declares it to be its purpose to provide access to legal representation for domestic violence victims in certain kinds of civil matters. The General Assembly finds that such representation can best be provided in an efficient, effective, and economic manner through established legal services programs in this State. (2004-186, s. 4.1.)

§ 7A-474.17. Definitions.

The following definitions shall apply throughout this Article, unless the context otherwise requires:

(1)   "Domestic violence victim" means a resident of North Carolina that has been subjected to acts of domestic violence as defined in G.S. 50B-1. A resident is not required to seek a protective order under Chapter 50B of the General Statutes to qualify as a domestic violence victim under this Article.

(2)   "Legal assistance" means the provision of any legal services, as defined by Chapter 84 of the General Statutes, consistent with this Article. Provided, that all legal services provided hereunder shall be performed consistently with the Rules of Professional Conduct promulgated by the North Carolina State Bar. Provided, further, that no funds appropriated under this Article shall be used for lobbying to influence the passage or defeat of any legislation before any municipal, county, state, or national legislative body.

(3)   "Established legal services program" means the following not-for-profit corporations using State funds to serve the counties listed: Pisgah Legal Services, serving Buncombe, Henderson, Madison, Polk, Rutherford, and Transylvania Counties; and Legal Aid of North Carolina; or any successor entity or entities of the named organizations, or, should any of the named organizations dissolve, the entity or entities providing substantially the same services in substantially the same service area. (2004-186, s. 4.1; 2008-194, s. 3(c).)

§ 7A-474.18. Eligible activities and limitations.

(a)   Eligible Activities. - Funds appropriated under this Article shall be used only for the following purposes:

(1)   To provide legal assistance to domestic violence victims.

(2)   To provide education to domestic violence victims regarding their rights and duties under the law.

(3)   To involve the private bar in the representation of domestic violence victims pursuant to this Article.

(b)   Eligible Cases. - The funds shall be prioritized by each legal services program to serve the greatest number of eligible clients, with emphasis placed on representation of clients needing legal assistance with proceedings pursuant to Chapter 50B of the General Statutes. Legal assistance shall be provided to eligible clients under this Article only in the following types of cases:

150

(1)   Actions for protective orders issued pursuant to Chapter 50B of the General Statutes;

(2)   Child custody and visitation issues; and

(3)   Legal services which ensure the safety of the client and the client's children.

(c)   Limitations. - No funds appropriated under this Article shall be used for any of the following purposes:

(1)   To provide legal assistance with respect to any criminal proceeding; or

(2)   To provide legal assistance to any prisoner within the Division of Adult Correction of the Department of Public Safety with regard to the terms of that person's incarceration. (2004-186, s. 4.1; 2011-145, s. 19.1(h); 2012-83, s. 16.)

§ 7A-474.19. Funds.

Funds to provide representation pursuant to this Article shall be provided to the North Carolina State Bar for provision of direct services by and support of the established legal services programs. The North Carolina State Bar shall allocate these funds directly to each of the established legal services programs with Pisgah Legal Services receiving the allocation for Buncombe, Henderson, Madison, Polk, Rutherford, and Transylvania Counties. Funds shall be allocated to each program based on the counties served by that program using the following formula:

(1)   Twenty percent (20%) based on a fixed equal dollar amount for each county.

(2)   Eighty percent (80%) based on the rate of civil actions filed pursuant to Chapter 50B of the General Statutes in that county.

The North Carolina State Bar shall not use any of these funds for its administrative costs. (2004-186, s. 4.1; 2008-194, s. 3(d).)

§ 7A-474.20. Records and reports.

The established legal services programs shall keep appropriate records and make periodic reports, as requested, to the North Carolina State Bar. The North Carolina State Bar shall report annually to the Chairs of the Joint Legislative Oversight Committee on Justice and Public Safety on the amount of the funds disbursed and the use of the funds by each legal services program receiving funds. The report to the Chairs of the Joint Legislative Oversight Committee on Justice and Public Safety shall be made by January 15 of each year beginning January 15, 2006. (2004-186, s. 4.1; 2013-360, s. 18B.5.)

Article 38.

Appellate Defender Office.

§§ 7A-475 through 7A-485: Expired.

Article 38A.

Appellate Defender Office.

§§ 7A-486 through 7A-486.7: Repealed by Session Laws 2000-144, s. 13, as amended by Session Laws 2001-424, s. 22.11(c), effective July 1, 2001.

§ 7A-487. Reserved for future codification purposes.

§ 7A-488. Reserved for future codification purposes.

Article 39.

Guardian Ad Litem Program.

§§ 7A-489 through 7A-493. Repealed by Session Laws 1998-202, s. 5, effective July 1, 1999.

Article 39A.

Custody and Visitation Mediation Program.

§ 7A-494. Custody and Visitation Mediation Program established.

(a)   The Administrative Office of the Courts shall establish a Custody and Visitation Mediation Program to provide statewide and uniform services in accordance with G.S. 50-13.1 in cases involving unresolved issues about the custody or visitation of minor children. The Director of the Administrative Office of the Courts shall appoint such AOC staff support required for planning, organizing, and administering such program on a statewide basis.

The purposes of the Custody and Visitation Mediation Program shall be to provide the services of skilled mediators to further the goals expressed in G.S. 50-13.1(b).

(b)   Beginning on July 1, 1989, the Administrative Office of the Courts shall establish in phases a statewide custody mediation program comprised of local district programs to be established in all judicial districts of the State. Each local district program shall consist of: a qualified mediator or mediators to provide mediation services; and such clerical staff as the Administrative Office of the Courts in consultation with the local district program deems necessary. Such personnel, to be employed by the Chief District Court Judge of the district, may serve as full-time or part-time State employees or, in the alternative, such activities may be provided on a contractual basis when determined appropriate by the Administrative Office of the Courts. The Administrative Office of the Courts may authorize all or part of a program in one judicial district to be operated in conjunction with that of another district or districts. The Director of the Administrative Office of the Courts is authorized to approve contractual agreements for such services as executed by order of the Chief District Court Judge of a district court district; such contracts to be exempt from competitive bidding procedures under Chapter 143 of the General Statutes. The Administrative Office of the Courts shall promulgate rules and regulations necessary and appropriate for the administration of the program. Funds appropriated by the General Assembly for the establishment and maintenance of mediation programs under this Article shall be administered by the Administrative Office of the Courts.

(c)   For a person to qualify to provide mediation services under this Article, that person shall show that he or she:

(1)   Has at minimum a master's degree in psychology, social work, family counselling, or a comparable human relations discipline; and

153

(2)   Has at least 40 hours of training in mediation techniques by a qualified instructor of mediation as determined by the Administrative Office of the Courts; and

(3)   Has had professional training and experience relating to child development, family dynamics, or comparable areas; and

(4)   Meets such other criteria as may be specified by the Administrative Office of the Courts. (1989, c. 795, s. 15.)

§ 7A-495. Implementation and administration.

(a)   Local District Program. - The Administrative Office of the Courts shall, in cooperation with each Chief District Court Judge and other district personnel, implement and administer the program mandated by this Article.

(b)   Advisory Committee Established. - The Director of the Administrative Office of the Courts shall appoint a Custody Mediation Advisory Committee consisting of at least five members to advise the Custody Mediation Program. The members of the Advisory Committee shall receive the same per diem and reimbursement for travel expenses as members of State boards and commissions generally. (1989, c. 795, s. 15.)

§ 7A-496. Reserved for future codification purposes.

§ 7A-497. Reserved for future codification purposes.

Article 39B.

Indigent Defense Services Act.

§ 7A-498. Title.

This Article shall be known and may be cited as the "Indigent Defense Services Act of 2000". (2000-144, s. 1.)

§ 7A-498.1. Purpose.

154

Whenever a person is determined to be indigent and entitled to counsel, it is the responsibility of the State under the federal and state constitutions to provide that person with counsel and the other necessary expenses of representation. The purpose of this Article is to:

(1)   Enhance oversight of the delivery of counsel and related services provided at State expense;

(2)   Improve the quality of representation and ensure the independence of counsel;

(3)   Establish uniform policies and procedures for the delivery of services;

(4)   Generate reliable statistical information in order to evaluate the services provided and funds expended; and

(5)   Deliver services in the most efficient and cost-effective manner without sacrificing quality representation. (2000-144, s. 1.)

§ 7A-498.2. Establishment of Office of Indigent Defense Services.

(a)   The Office of Indigent Defense Services, which is administered by the Director of Indigent Defense Services and includes the Commission on Indigent Defense Services and the Sentencing Services Program established in Article 61 of this Chapter, is created within the Judicial Department. As used in this Article, "Office" means the Office of Indigent Defense Services, "Director" means the Director of Indigent Defense Services, and "Commission" means the Commission on Indigent Defense Services.

(b)   The Office of Indigent Defense Services shall exercise its prescribed powers independently of the head of the Administrative Office of the Courts. The Office may enter into contracts, own property, and accept funds, grants, and gifts from any public or private source to pay expenses incident to implementing its purposes.

(c)   The Director of the Administrative Office of the Courts shall provide general administrative support to the Office of Indigent Defense Services. The term "general administrative support" includes purchasing, payroll, and similar administrative services.

(d)   The budget of the Office of Indigent Defense Services shall be a part of the Judicial Department's budget. The Commission on Indigent Defense Services shall consult with the Director of the Administrative Office of the Courts, who shall assist the Commission in preparing and presenting to the General Assembly the Office's budget, but the Commission shall have the final authority with respect to preparation of the Office's budget and with respect to representation of matters pertaining to the Office before the General Assembly.

(e)   The Director of the Administrative Office of the Courts shall not reduce or modify the budget of the Office of Indigent Defense Services or use funds appropriated to the Office without the approval of the Commission. (2000-144, s. 1; 2002-126, s. 14.7(b).)

§ 7A-498.3. Responsibilities of Office of Indigent Defense Services.

(a)   The Office of Indigent Defense Services shall be responsible for establishing, supervising, and maintaining a system for providing legal representation and related services in the following cases:

(1)   Cases in which an indigent person is subject to a deprivation of liberty or other constitutionally protected interest and is entitled by law to legal representation;

(2)   Cases in which an indigent person is entitled to legal representation under G.S. 7A-451 and G.S. 7A-451.1;

(2a)   Cases in which the State is legally obligated to provide legal assistance and access to the courts to inmates in the custody of the Division of Adult Correction of the Department of Public Safety; and

(3)   Any other cases in which the Office of Indigent Defense Services is designated by statute as responsible for providing legal representation.

(b)   The Office of Indigent Defense Services shall develop policies and procedures for determining indigency in cases subject to this Article, and those policies shall be applied uniformly throughout the State. Except in cases under subdivision (2a) of subsection (a) of this section, the court shall determine in each case whether a person is indigent and entitled to legal representation, and counsel shall be appointed as provided in G.S. 7A-452.

156

(c)   In all cases subject to this Article, appointment of counsel, determination of compensation, appointment of experts, and use of funds for experts and other services related to legal representation shall be in accordance with rules and procedures adopted by the Office of Indigent Defense Services.

(d)   The Office of Indigent Defense Services shall allocate and disburse funds appropriated for legal representation and related services in cases subject to this Article pursuant to rules and procedures established by the Office. (2000-144, s. 1; 2005-276, s. 14.9(a); 2011-145, s. 19.1(h).)

§ 7A-498.4. Establishment of Commission on Indigent Defense Services.

(a)   The Commission on Indigent Defense Services is created within the Office of Indigent Defense Services and shall consist of 13 members. To create an effective working group, assure continuity, and achieve staggered terms, the Commission shall be appointed as provided in this section.

(b)   The members of the Commission shall be appointed as follows:

(1)   The Chief Justice of the North Carolina Supreme Court shall appoint one member, who shall be an active or former member of the North Carolina judiciary.

(2)   The Governor shall appoint one member, who shall be a nonattorney.

(3)   The General Assembly shall appoint one member, who shall be an attorney, upon the recommendation of the President Pro Tempore of the Senate.

(4)   The General Assembly shall appoint one member, who shall be an attorney, upon the recommendation of the Speaker of the House of Representatives.

(5)   The North Carolina Public Defenders Association shall appoint member, who shall be an attorney.

(6)   The North Carolina State Bar shall appoint one member, who shall be an attorney.

(7)   The North Carolina Bar Association shall appoint one member, who shall be an attorney.

(8)   The North Carolina Academy of Trial Lawyers shall appoint one member, who shall be an attorney.

(9)   The North Carolina Association of Black Lawyers shall appoint one member, who shall be an attorney.

(10)   The North Carolina Association of Women Lawyers shall appoint one member, who shall be an attorney.

(11)   The Commission shall appoint three members, who shall reside in different judicial districts from one another. One appointee shall be a nonattorney, and one appointee may be an active member of the North Carolina judiciary. One appointee shall be Native American. The initial three members satisfying this subdivision shall be appointed as provided in subsection (k) of this section.

(c)   The terms of members appointed pursuant to subsection (b) of this section shall be as follows:

(1)   The initial appointments by the Chief Justice, the Governor, and the General Assembly shall be for four years.

(2)   The initial appointments by the Public Defenders Association and State Bar, and one appointment by the Commission, shall be for three years.

(3)   The initial appointments by the Bar Association and Trial Academy, and one appointment by the Commission, shall be for two years.

(4)   The initial appointments by the Black Lawyers Association and Women Lawyers Association, and one appointment by the Commission, shall be for one year.

At the expiration of these initial terms, appointments shall be for four years and shall be made by the appointing authorities designated in subsection (b) of this section. No person shall serve more than two consecutive four-year terms plus any initial term of less than four years.

(d)   Persons appointed to the Commission shall have significant experience in the defense of criminal or other cases subject to this Article or shall have demonstrated a strong commitment to quality representation in indigent defense matters. No active prosecutors or law enforcement officials, or active employees of such persons, may be appointed to or serve on the Commission. No active judicial officials, or active employees of such persons, may be appointed to or serve on the Commission, except as provided in subsection (b) of this section. No active public defenders, active employees of public defenders, or other active employees of the Office of Indigent Defense Services may be appointed to or serve on the Commission, except that notwithstanding this subsection, G.S. 14-234, or any other provision of law, Commission members may include part-time public defenders employed by the Office of Indigent Defense Services and may include persons, or employees of persons or organizations, who provide legal services subject to this Article as contractors or appointed attorneys.

(e)   All members of the Commission are entitled to vote on any matters coming before the Commission unless otherwise provided by rules adopted by the Commission concerning voting on matters in which a member has, or appears to have, a financial or other personal interest.

(f)   Each member of the Commission shall serve until a successor in office has been appointed. Vacancies shall be filled by appointment by the appointing authority for the unexpired term. Removal of Commission members shall be in accordance with policies and procedures adopted by the Commission.

(g)   A quorum for purposes of conducting Commission business shall be a majority of the members of the Commission.

(h)   The Commission shall elect a Commission chair from the members of the Commission for a term of two years.

(i)   The Director of Indigent Defense Services shall attend all Commission meetings except those relating to removal or reappointment of the Director or allegations of misconduct by the Director. The Director shall not vote on any matter decided by the Commission.

(j)   Commission members shall not receive compensation but are entitled to be paid necessary subsistence and travel expenses in accordance with G.S. 138-5 and G.S. 138-6 as applicable.

(k)   The Commission shall hold its first meeting no later than September 15, 2000. All appointments to the Commission specified in subdivisions (1) through (10) of subsection (b) of this section shall be made by the appointing authorities by September 1, 2000. The appointee of the Chief Justice shall convene the first meeting. No later than 30 days after its first meeting, the Commission shall make the appointments specified in subdivision (11) of subsection (b) of this section and shall elect its chair. (2000-144, s. 1; 2001-424, s. 22.11(b).)

§ 7A-498.5. Responsibilities of Commission.

(a)   The Commission shall have as its principal purpose the development and improvement of programs by which the Office of Indigent Defense Services provides legal representation to indigent persons.

(b)   The Commission shall appoint the Director of the Office of Indigent Defense Services, who shall be chosen on the basis of training, experience, and other qualifications. The Commission shall consult with the Chief Justice and Director of the Administrative Office of the Courts in selecting a Director, but shall have final authority in making the appointment.

(c)   The Commission shall develop standards governing the provision of services under this Article. The standards shall include:

(1)   Standards for maintaining and operating regional and district public defender offices and appellate defender offices, including requirements regarding qualifications, training, and size of the legal and supporting staff;

(2)   Standards prescribing minimum experience, training, and other qualifications for appointed counsel;

(3)   Standards for public defender and appointed counsel caseloads;

(4)   Standards for the performance of public defenders and appointed counsel;

(5)   Standards for the independent, competent, and efficient representation of clients whose cases present conflicts of interest, in both the trial and appellate courts;

160

(6)   Standards for providing and compensating experts and others who provide services related to legal representation;

(7)   Standards for qualifications and performance in capital cases, consistent with any rules adopted by the Supreme Court; and

(8)   Standards for determining indigency and for assessing and collecting the costs of legal representation and related services.

(d)   The Commission shall determine the methods for delivering legal services to indigent persons eligible for legal representation under this Article and shall establish in each district or combination of districts a system of appointed counsel, contract counsel, part-time public defenders, public defender offices, appellate defender services, and other methods for delivering counsel services, or any combination of these services.

(e)   In determining the method of services to be provided in a particular district, the Director shall consult with the district bar as defined in G.S. 84-19 and the judges of the district or districts under consideration. The Commission shall adopt procedures ensuring that affected local bars have the opportunity to be significantly involved in determining the method or methods for delivering services in their districts. The Commission shall solicit written comments from the affected local district bar, senior resident superior court judge, and chief district court judge. Those comments, along with the recommendations of the Commission, shall be forwarded to the members of the General Assembly who represent the affected district and to other interested parties.

(f)   The Commission shall establish policies and procedures with respect to the distribution of funds appropriated under this Article, including rates of compensation for appointed counsel, schedules of allowable expenses, appointment and compensation of expert witnesses, and procedures for applying for and receiving compensation. The rate of compensation set for expert witnesses may be no greater than the rate set by the Administrative Office of the Courts under G.S. 7A-314(d).

(g)   The Commission shall approve and recommend to the General Assembly a budget for the Office of Indigent Defense Services.

(h)   The Commission shall adopt such other rules and procedures as it deems necessary for the conduct of business by the Commission and the Office of Indigent Defense Services. (2000-144, s. 1; 2001-392, s. 2; 2011-145, s. 15.20.)

§ 7A-498.6. Director of Indigent Defense Services.

(a)   The Director of Indigent Defense Services shall be appointed by the Commission for a term of four years. The salary of the Director shall be set by the General Assembly in the Current Operations Appropriations Act, after consultation with the Commission. The Director may be removed during this term in the discretion of the Commission by a vote of two-thirds of all of the Commission members. The Director shall be an attorney licensed and eligible to practice in the courts of this State at the time of appointment and at all times during service as the Director.

(b)   The Director shall:

(1)   Prepare and submit to the Commission a proposed budget for the Office of Indigent Defense Services, an annual report containing pertinent data on the operations, costs, and needs of the Office, and such other information as the Commission may require;

(2)   Assist the Commission in developing rules and standards for the delivery of services under this Article;

(3)   Administer and coordinate the operations of the Office and supervise compliance with standards adopted by the Commission;

(4)   Subject to policies and procedures established by the Commission, hire such professional, technical, and support personnel as deemed reasonably necessary for the efficient operation of the Office of Indigent Defense Services;

(5)   Keep and maintain proper financial records for use in calculating the costs of the operations of the Office of Indigent Defense Services;

(6)   Apply for and accept on behalf of the Office of Indigent Defense Services any funds that may become available from government grants, private gifts, donations, or devises from any source;

(7)   Coordinate the services of the Office of Indigent Defense Services with any federal, county, or private programs established to provide assistance to

indigent persons in cases subject to this Article and consult with professional bodies concerning improving the administration of indigent services;

(8)   Conduct training programs for attorneys and others involved in the legal representation of persons subject to this Article;

(8a)   Administer the Sentencing Services Program established in Article 61 of this Chapter; and

(9)   Perform other duties as the Commission may assign.

(c)   In lieu of merit and other increment raises paid to regular State employees, the Director of Indigent Defense Services shall receive as longevity pay an amount equal to four and eight-tenths percent (4.8%) of the annual salary set forth in the Current Operations Appropriations Act payable monthly after five years of service, nine and six-tenths percent (9.6%) after 10 years of service, fourteen and four-tenths percent (14.4%) after 15 years of service, nineteen and two-tenths percent (19.2%) after 20 years of service, and twenty-four percent (24%) after 25 years of service. "Service" means service as Director of Indigent Defense Services, a public defender, appellate defender, assistant public or appellate defender, district attorney, assistant district attorney, justice or judge of the General Court of Justice, or clerk of superior court. (2000-144, s. 1; 2002-126, s. 14.7(c); 2008-107, ss. 26.4(b), (c); 2011-284, s. 7.)

§ 7A-498.7. Public Defender Offices.

(a)   The following counties of the State are organized into the defender districts listed below, and in each of those defender districts an office of public defender is established:

Defender District		Counties
1 Currituck,	Dare, Gates, Pasquotank,	Camden, Chowan,
		Perquimans
3A		Pitt

163

3B	Carteret
5	New Hanover
10	Wake
12	Cumberland
14	Durham
15B	Orange, Chatham
16A	Scotland, Hoke
16B	Robeson
18	Guilford
21	Forsyth
26	Mecklenburg
27A	Gaston
28	Buncombe
29B Transylvania	Henderson, Polk,

After notice to, and consultation with, the affected district bar, senior resident superior court judge, and chief district court judge, the Commission on Indigent Defense Services may recommend to the General Assembly that a district or regional public defender office be established. A legislative act is required in order to establish a new office or to abolish an existing office.

(b)   For each new term, and to fill any vacancy, public defenders shall be appointed from a list of not less than two and not more than three names nominated by written ballot of the attorneys resident in the defender district who are licensed to practice law in North Carolina. The balloting shall be conducted pursuant to rules adopted by the Commission on Indigent Defense Services. The appointment shall be made by the senior resident superior court judge of

164

the superior court district or set of districts as defined in G.S. 7A-41.1 that includes the county or counties of the defender district for which the public defender is being appointed.

(c)   A public defender shall be an attorney licensed to practice law in North Carolina and shall devote full time to the duties of the office. In lieu of merit and other increment raises paid to regular State employees, a public defender shall receive as longevity pay an amount equal to four and eight-tenths percent (4.8%) of the annual salary set forth in the Current Operations Appropriations Act payable monthly after five years of service, nine and six-tenths percent (9.6%) after 10 years of service, fourteen and four-tenths percent (14.4%) after 15 years of service, nineteen and two-tenths percent (19.2%) after 20 years of service, and twenty-four percent (24%) after 25 years of service. "Service" means service as a public defender, appellate defender, assistant public or appellate defender, district attorney, assistant district attorney, justice or judge of the General Court of Justice, or clerk of superior court.

(c1)   When traveling on official business, each public defender and assistant public defender is entitled to reimbursement for his or her subsistence expenses to the same extent as State employees generally. When traveling on official business outside his or her county of residence, each public defender and assistant public defender is entitled to reimbursement for travel expenses to the same extent as State employees generally. For purposes of this subsection, the term "official business" does not include regular, daily commuting between a person's home and the public defender's office. Travel distances, for purposes of reimbursement for mileage, shall be determined according to the travel policy of the Administrative Office of the Courts.

(d)   Subject to standards adopted by the Commission, the day-to-day operation and administration of public defender offices shall be the responsibility of the public defender in charge of the office. The public defender shall keep appropriate records and make periodic reports, as requested, to the Director of the Office of Indigent Defense Services on matters related to the operation of the office.

(e)   The Office of Indigent Defense Services shall procure office equipment and supplies for the public defender, and provide secretarial and library support from State funds appropriated to the public defender's office for this purpose.

(f)   Each public defender is entitled to assistant public defenders, investigators, and other staff, full-time or part-time, as may be authorized by the

Commission. Assistants, investigators, and other staff are appointed by the public defender and serve at the pleasure of the public defender. Average and minimum compensation of assistants shall be as provided in the biennial Current Operations Appropriations Act. The actual salaries of assistants shall be set by the public defender in charge of the office, subject to approval by the Commission. The Commission shall fix the compensation of investigators. Assistants and investigators shall perform such duties as may be assigned by the public defender.

(f1)   In cases in which a public defender determines that a conflict of interest exists in the office, whenever practical, rather than obtaining private assigned counsel to resolve the conflict, the public defender may request the appointment of an assistant public defender from another office of public defender in the region to resolve the conflict.

(g)   In lieu of merit and other increment raises paid to regular State employees, an assistant public defender shall receive as longevity pay an amount equal to four and eight-tenths percent (4.8%) of the annual salary set forth in the Current Operations Appropriations Act payable monthly after five years of service, nine and six-tenths percent (9.6%) after 10 years of service, fourteen and four-tenths percent (14.4%) after 15 years of service, nineteen and two-tenths percent (19.2%) after 20 years of service, and twenty-four percent (24%) after 25 years of service. "Service" means service as a public defender, appellate defender, assistant public or appellate defender, district attorney, assistant district attorney, justice or judge of the General Court of Justice, or clerk of superior court.

(h)   The term of office of public defender appointed under this section is four years. A public defender or assistant public defender may be suspended or removed from office, and reinstated, for the same causes and under the same procedures as are applicable to removal of a district attorney.

(i)   A public defender may apply to the Director of the Office of Indigent Defense Services to enter into contracts with local governments for the provision by the State of services of temporary assistant public defenders pursuant to G.S. 153A-212.1 or G.S. 160A-289.1.

(j)   The Director of the Office of Indigent Defense Services may provide assistance requested pursuant to subsection (i) of this section only upon a showing by the requesting public defender, supported by facts, that the overwhelming public interest warrants the use of additional resources for the

166

speedy disposition of cases involving drug offenses, domestic violence, or other offenses involving a threat to public safety.

(k)   The terms of any contract entered into with local governments pursuant to subsection (i) of this section shall be fixed by the Director of the Office of Indigent Defense Services in each case. Nothing in this section shall be construed to obligate the General Assembly to make any appropriation to implement the provisions of this section or to obligate the Office of Indigent Defense Services to provide the administrative costs of establishing or maintaining the positions or services provided for under this section. Further, nothing in this section shall be construed to obligate the Office of Indigent Defense Services to maintain positions or services initially provided for under this section. (2000-144, s. 1; 2001-424, ss. 22.11(a), 22.11(d); 2002-126, s. 14.11(a); 2003-284, ss. 30.19A(c), (d); 2004-124, ss. 14.4(a), (b); 2005-276, s. 14.14(a); 2005-345, s. 50A; 2007-323, ss. 14.4(d), 28.18A(g); 2009-451, s. 15.17B(c); 2010-96, s. 27; 2011-145, s. 15.16(b); 2013-360, ss. 18A.5(a), 18A6(a).)

§ 7A-498.8. Appellate Defender.

(a)   The appellate defender shall be appointed by the Commission on Indigent Defense Services for a term of four years. A vacancy in the office of appellate defender shall be filled by appointment of the Commission on Indigent Defense Services for the unexpired term. The appellate defender may be suspended or removed from office for cause by two-thirds vote of all the members of the Commission on Indigent Defense Services. The Commission shall provide the appellate defender with timely written notice of the alleged causes and an opportunity for hearing before the Commission prior to taking any final action to remove or suspend the appellate defender, and the appellate defender shall be given written notice of the Commission's decision. The appellate defender may obtain judicial review of suspension or removal by the Commission by filing a petition within 30 days of receiving notice of the decision with the Superior Court of Wake County. Review of the Commission's decision shall be heard on the record and not as a de novo review or trial de novo. The Commission shall adopt rules implementing this section.

(b)   The appellate defender shall perform such duties as may be directed by the Office of Indigent Defense Services, including:

(1)   Representing indigent persons subsequent to conviction in trial courts. The Office of Indigent Defense Services may, following consultation with the appellate defender and consistent with the resources available to the appellate defender to ensure quality criminal defense services by the appellate defender's office, assign appeals, or authorize the appellate defender to assign appeals, to a local public defender's office or to private assigned counsel.

(2)   Maintaining a clearinghouse of materials and a repository of briefs prepared by the appellate defender to be made available to private counsel representing indigents in criminal cases.

(3)   Providing continuing legal education training to assistant appellate defenders and to private counsel representing indigents in criminal cases, including capital cases, as resources are available.

(4)   Providing consulting services to attorneys representing defendants in capital cases.

(5)   Recruiting qualified members of the private bar who are willing to provide representation in State and federal death penalty postconviction proceedings.

(6)   In the appellate defender's discretion, serving as counsel of record for indigent defendants in capital cases in State court.

(6a)   In the appellate defender's discretion, serving as counsel of record for indigent defendants in the United States Supreme Court pursuant to a petition for writ of certiorari of the decision on direct appeal by a court of the North Carolina Appellate Division.

(7)   Undertaking other direct representation and consultation in capital cases pending in federal court only to the extent that such work is fully federally funded.

(c)   The appellate defender shall appoint assistants and staff, not to exceed the number authorized by the Office of Indigent Defense Services. The assistants and staff shall serve at the pleasure of the appellate defender.

(d)   Funds to operate the office of appellate defender, including office space, office equipment, supplies, postage, telephone, library, staff salaries, training, and travel, shall be provided by the Office of Indigent Defense Services from

168

funds authorized by law. Salaries shall be set by the Office of Indigent Defense Services. (2000-144, s. 1; 2007-323, s. 14.19(b); 2008-187, s. 3.)

§ 7A-499. Reserved for future codification purposes.

SUBCHAPTER X. NORTH CAROLINA COURTS COMMISSION.

Article 40.

North Carolina Courts Commission.

§§ 7A-500 through 7A-505: Repealed by Session Laws 1975, c. 956, s. 18.

Article 40A.

North Carolina Courts Commission.

§ 7A-506. Creation; members; terms; qualifications; vacancies.

(a)   The North Carolina Courts Commission is created. Effective July 1, 1993, it shall consist of 28 members, seven to be appointed by the Governor, seven to be appointed by the Speaker of the House of Representatives, seven to be appointed by the President Pro Tempore of the Senate, and seven to be appointed by the Chief Justice of the Supreme Court.

(b)   Of the appointees of the Chief Justice of the Supreme Court, one shall be a Justice of the Supreme Court, one shall be a Judge of the Court of Appeals, two shall be judges of superior court, two shall be district court judges, and one shall be a public member who is not an attorney and who is not an officer or employee of the Judicial Department.

(c)   Of the seven appointees of the Governor, one shall be a district attorney, one shall be a practicing attorney, one shall be a clerk of superior court, at least three shall be members of the General Assembly, at least two shall not be attorneys, and of the nonattorneys, one shall be a public member who is not an officer or employee of the Judicial Department.

(d)   Of the seven appointees of the Speaker of the House, at least three shall be practicing attorneys, at least three shall be members of the General Assembly, at least two shall not be attorneys, and of the non-attorneys, one shall be a public member who is not an officer or employee of the Judicial Department.

(e)   Of the seven appointees of the President Pro Tempore of the Senate, at least three shall be practicing attorneys, at least three shall be members of the General Assembly, at least one shall be a magistrate, and one shall be a public member who is not an attorney and who is not an officer or employee of the Judicial Department.

(f)   Of the initial appointments of each appointing authority, three shall be appointed for four-year terms to begin July 1, 1993, and three shall be appointed for two-year terms to begin July 1, 1993. The two public members appointed by the Governor and the Speaker of the House of Representatives shall be appointed for four-year terms to begin July 1, 1997. The two public members appointed by the Chief Justice and the President Pro Tempore of the Senate shall be appointed for two-year terms to begin July 1, 1997. Successors shall be appointed for four-year terms.

(g)   A vacancy in membership shall be filled for the remainder of the unexpired term by the appointing authority who made the original appointment. A member whose term expires may be reappointed. (1979, c. 1077, s. 1; 1981, c. 847; 1981 (Reg. Sess., 1982), c. 1253, s. 4; 1983, c. 181, ss. 1, 2; c. 774, s. 2; 1991, c. 739, s. 7; 1993, c. 438, s. 1; 1997-82, s. 1.)

§ 7A-507. Ex officio members.

The following additional members shall serve ex officio: the Administrative Officer of the Courts; a representative of the N.C. State Bar appointed by the Council thereof; and a representative of the N.C. Bar Association appointed by the Board of Governors thereof. The Administrative Officer of the Courts has no vote. (1979, c. 1077, s. 1; 1997-82, s. 2.)

§ 7A-508. Duties.

It shall be the duty of the Commission to make continuing studies of the structure, organization, jurisdiction, procedures and personnel of the Judicial Department and of the General Court of Justice and to make recommendations to the General Assembly for such changes therein as will facilitate the administration of justice. (1979, c. 1077, s. 1.)

§ 7A-509. Chair; meetings; compensation of members.

The Governor, after consultation with the Chief Justice of the Supreme Court, shall appoint a chair from the legislative members of the Commission. The term of the chair is two years, and the chair may be reappointed. The Commission shall meet at such times and places as the chair shall designate. The facilities of the State Legislative Building shall be available to the Commission, subject to approval of the Legislative Services Commission. The members of the Commission shall receive the same per diem and reimbursement for travel expenses as members of State boards and commissions generally. (1979, c. 1077, s. 1; 1993, c. 438, s. 2.)

§ 7A-510. Supporting services.

The Commission is authorized to contract for such professional and clerical services as are necessary in the proper performance of its duties. (1979, c. 1077, s. 1.)

§§ 7A-511 through 7A-515. Reserved for future codification purposes.

subchapter xi. north carolina juvenile code.

Article 41.

Purpose; Definitions.

§§ 7A-516 through 7A-522. Repealed by Session Laws 1998-202, s. 5.

Article 42.

Jurisdiction.

§§ 7A-523 through 7A-529. Repealed by Session Laws 1998-202, s. 5.

Article 43.

Screening of Delinquency and Undisciplined Petitions.

§§ 7A-530 through 7A-541. Repealed by Session Laws 1998-202, s. 5.

Article 44.

Screening of Abuse and Neglect Complaints.

§§ 7A-542 through 7A-557. Repealed by Session Laws 1998-202, s. 5.

Article 45.

Venue; Petition; Summons.

§§ 7A-558 through 7A-570. Repealed by Session Laws 1998-202, s. 5.

Article 46.

Temporary Custody; Secure and Nonsecure Custody; Custody Hearings.

§§ 7A-571 through 7A-577. Repealed by Session Laws 1998-202, s. 5.

§ 7A-577.1. Recodified as § 7B-507.

§§ 7A-578 through 7A-583. Repealed by Session Laws 1998-202, s. 5.

Article 47.

Basic Rights.

§§ 7A-584 through 7A-593. Repealed by Session Laws 1998-202, s. 5.

Article 48.

Law-Enforcement Procedures in Delinquency Proceedings.

172

§§ 7A-594 through 7A-607. Repealed by Session Laws 1998-202, s. 5.

Article 49.

Transfer to Superior Court.

§§ 7A-608 through 7A-617. Repealed by Session Laws 1998-202, s. 5.

Article 50.

Discovery.

§§ 7A-618 through 7A-626. Repealed by Session Laws 1998-202, s. 5.

Article 51.

Hearing Procedures.

§§ 7A-627 through 7A-645. Repealed by Session Laws 1998-202, s. 5.

Article 52.

Dispositions.

§§ 7A-646 through 7A-657. Repealed by Session Laws 1998-202, s. 5.

§ 7A-657.1. Recodified as § 7B-907.

 §§ 7A-658 through 7A-663. Repealed by Session Laws 1998-202, s. 5.

Article 53.

Modification and Enforcement of Dispositional Orders; Appeals.

§§ 7A-664 through 7A-674. Repealed by Session Laws 1998-202, s. 5.

Article 54.

Juvenile Records and Social Reports.

§§ 7A-675 through 7A-683. Repealed by Session Laws 1998-202, s. 5.

Article 55.

Interstate Compact on Juveniles.

§§ 7A-684 through 7A-716. Repealed by Session Laws 1998-202, s. 5.

Article 56.

Emancipation.

§§ 7A-717 through 7A-731. Repealed by Session Laws 1998-202, s. 5.

Article 57.

Judicial Consent for Emergency Surgical or Medical Treatment.

§§ 7A-732 through 7A-739. Repealed by Session Laws 1998-202, s. 5.

Article 58.

Juvenile Law Study Commission.

§§ 7A-740 through 7A-744. Repealed by Session Laws 1998-202, s. 5.

Article 59.

§§ 7A-745 through 7A-749. Repealed by Session Laws 1998-202, s. 5.

SUBCHAPTER XII. ADMINISTRATIVE HEARINGS.

Article 60.

Office of Administrative Hearings.

§ 7A-750. Creation; status; purpose.

There is created an Office of Administrative Hearings. The Office of Administrative Hearings is an independent, quasi-judicial agency under Article III, Sec. 11 of the Constitution and, in accordance with Article IV, Sec. 3 of the Constitution, has such judicial powers as may be reasonably necessary as an incident to the accomplishment of the purposes for which it is created. The Office of Administrative Hearings is established to ensure that administrative decisions are made in a fair and impartial manner to protect the due process rights of citizens who challenge administrative action and to provide a source of independent administrative law judges to conduct administrative hearings in contested cases in accordance with Chapter 150B of the General Statutes and thereby prevent the commingling of legislative, executive, and judicial functions in the administrative process. It shall also maintain dockets and records of contested cases and shall codify and publish all administrative rules. (1985, c. 746, s. 2; 1991, c. 103, s. 1; 2000-190, s. 2.)

§ 7A-751. Agency head; powers and duties; salaries of Chief Administrative Law Judge and other administrative law judges.

(a)   The head of the Office of Administrative Hearings is the Chief Administrative Law Judge, who shall serve as Director of the Office. The Chief Administrative Law Judge has the powers and duties conferred on that position by this Chapter and the Constitution and laws of this State and may adopt rules to implement the conferred powers and duties.

The salary of the Chief Administrative Law Judge shall be the same as that fixed from time to time for district court judges. The salary of a Senior Administrative Law Judge shall be ninety-five percent (95%) of the salary of the Chief Administrative Law Judge.

In lieu of merit and other increment raises, the Chief Administrative Law Judge and any Senior Administrative Law Judge shall receive longevity pay on the

175

same basis as is provided to employees of the State who are subject to the North Carolina Human Resources Act.

(b)   The salary of other administrative law judges shall be ninety percent (90%) of the salary of the Chief Administrative Law Judge.

In lieu of merit and other increment raises, an administrative law judge shall receive longevity pay on the same basis as is provided to employees who are subject to the North Carolina Human Resources Act. (1985, c. 746, s. 2; 1987, c. 774, s. 1; c. 827, s. 1; 1987 (Reg. Sess., 1988), c. 1100, s. 16(b); c. 1111, s. 14(b); 1989, c. 500, s. 45; 1991, c. 103, s. 1; 1997-34, s. 11; 1997-443, s. 33.8; 2000-140, s. 38; 2013-382, s. 9.1(c).)

§ 7A-752. Chief Administrative Law Judge; appointments; vacancy.

The Chief Administrative Law Judge of the Office of Administrative Hearings shall be appointed by the Chief Justice for a term of office of four years. The first Chief Administrative Law Judge shall be appointed as soon as practicable for a term to begin on the day of his appointment and to end on June 30, 1989. Successors to the first Chief Administrative Law Judge shall be appointed for a term to begin on July 1 of the year the preceding term ends and to end on June 30 four years later. A Chief Administrative Law Judge may continue to serve beyond his term until his successor is duly appointed and sworn, but any holdover shall not affect the expiration date of the succeeding term.

The Chief Administrative Law Judge shall designate one administrative law judge as senior administrative law judge. The senior administrative law judge may perform the duties of Chief Administrative Law Judge if the Chief Administrative Law Judge is absent or unable to serve temporarily for any reason. (1985, c. 746, s. 2; 1985 (Reg. Sess., 1986), c. 1022, ss. 3, 6(2), 6(3); 1987 (Reg. Sess., 1988), c. 1111, ss. 15, 25; 1991, c. 103, s. 1.)

§ 7A-753. Additional administrative law judges; appointment; specialization.

The Chief Administrative Law Judge shall appoint additional administrative law judges to serve in the Office of Administrative Hearings in such numbers as the General Assembly provides. No person shall be appointed or designated an administrative law judge except as provided in this Article.

The Chief Administrative Law Judge may designate certain administrative law judges as having the experience and expertise to preside at specific types of contested cases and assign only these designated administrative law judges to preside at those cases. (1985, c. 746, s. 2; 1985 (Reg. Sess., 1986), c. 1022, ss. 4, 6(2); 1987 (Reg. Sess., 1988), c. 1111, ss. 24, 25; 1991, c. 103, s. 1.)

§ 7A-754. Qualifications; standards of conduct; removal.

Only persons duly authorized to practice law in the General Court of Justice shall be eligible for appointment as the Director and chief administrative law judge or as an administrative law judge in the Office of Administrative Hearings. The Chief Administrative Law Judge and the administrative law judges shall comply with the Model Code of Judicial Conduct for State Administrative Law Judges, as adopted by the National Conference of Administrative Law Judges, Judicial Division, American Bar Association, (revised August 1998), as amended from time to time, except that the provisions of this section shall control as to the private practice of law in lieu of Canon 4G, and G.S. 126-13 shall control as to political activity in lieu of Canon 5. Failure to comply with the applicable provisions of the Model Code may constitute just cause for disciplinary action under Chapter 126 of the General Statutes and grounds for removal from office. Neither the chief administrative law judge nor any administrative law judge may engage in the private practice of law as defined in G.S. 84-2.1 while in office; violation of this provision shall constitute just cause for disciplinary action under Chapter 126 of the General Statutes and shall be grounds for removal from office. Each administrative law judge shall take the oaths required by Chapter 11 of the General Statutes. An administrative law judge may be removed from office by the Director of the Office of Administrative Hearings for just cause, as that term is used in G.S. 126-35 and this section. (1985, c. 746, s. 2; 1985 (Reg. Sess., 1986), c. 1022, s. 6(1), 6(3); 1991, c. 103, s. 1; 2000-190, s. 3.)
§ 7A-755. Expenses reimbursed.

The Chief Administrative Law Judge of the Office of Administrative Hearings and all administrative law judges shall be reimbursed for travel and subsistence expenses at the rates allowed to State officers and employees by G.S. 138-6(a). (1985, c. 746, s. 2; 1985 (Reg. Sess., 1986), c. 1022, s. 6(2); 1987 (Reg. Sess., 1988), c. 1111, s. 25; 1991, c. 103, s. 1.)

§ 7A-756. Power to administer oaths and issue subpoenas.

The chief administrative law judge and all administrative law judges in the Office of Administrative Hearings may, in connection with any pending or potential contested case under Chapter 150B:

(1)   Administer oaths and affirmations;

(2)   Sign and issue subpoenas in the name of the Office of Administrative Hearings requiring attendance and giving of testimony by witnesses and the production of books, papers, and other documentary evidence; and

(3)   Apply to the General Court of Justice, Superior Court Division, for any order necessary to enforce the powers conferred in this Article. (1985, c. 746, s. 2; 1985 (Reg. Sess., 1986), c. 1022, s. 6(1), 6(2); 1987, c. 827, s. 1; 1991, c. 103, s. 1.)

§ 7A-757. Temporary administrative law judges; appointments; powers and standards; fees.

When regularly appointed administrative law judges are unavailable, the Chief Administrative Law Judge of the Office of Administrative Hearings may contract with qualified individuals to serve as administrative law judges for specific assignments. A temporary administrative law judge shall have the same powers and adhere to the same standards as a regular administrative law judge in the conduct of a hearing. A temporary administrative law judge shall not be considered a State employee by virtue of this assignment, and shall be remunerated for his service at a rate not to exceed three hundred dollars ($300.00) per day and shall be reimbursed for travel and subsistence expenses at the rate allowed to State officers and employees by G.S. 138-6(a). The Chief Administrative Law Judge may also designate a full-time State employee to serve as a temporary administrative law judge with the consent of the employee and his supervisor; however, the employee is not entitled to any additional pay for this service. (1985, c. 746, s. 2; 1985 (Reg. Sess., 1986), c. 1022, s. 5; 1987, c. 878, s. 14; 1987 (Reg. Sess., 1988), c. 1111, s. 25; 1991, c. 103, s. 1.)

§ 7A-758. Availability of administrative law judge to exempt agencies.

The Chief Administrative Law Judge of the Office of Administrative Hearings may, upon request of the head of the agency, provide an administrative law judge to preside at hearings of public bodies not otherwise authorized or required by statute to utilize an administrative law judge from the Office of Administrative Hearings including, but not limited to, State agencies exempt from the provisions of Chapter 150B, municipal corporations or other subdivisions of the State, and agencies of such subdivisions. (1985, c. 746, s. 2; 1987, c. 827, s. 1, c. 878, s. 15; 1987 (Reg. Sess., 1988), c. 1111, s. 25; 1991, c 103, s. 1.)

§ 7A-759. Role as deferral agency.

(a)   The Office of Administrative Hearings is designated to serve as the State's deferral agency for cases deferred by the Equal Employment Opportunity Commission to the Office of Administrative Hearings as provided in Section 706 of the Civil Rights Act of 1964, 42 U.S.C. § 2000e-5, the Age Discrimination in Employment Act, 29 U.S.C. § 621 et seq., and the Americans with Disabilities Act, 42 U.S.C. § 12101 et seq. for charges filed by State or local government employees covered under Chapter 126 of the General Statutes and shall have all of the powers and authority necessary to function as a deferral agency.

(b)   The Chief Administrative Law Judge is authorized and directed to contract with the Equal Employment Opportunity Commission for the Office of Administrative Hearings to serve as a deferral agency and to establish and maintain a Civil Rights Division in the Office of Administrative Hearings to carry out the functions of a deferral agency.

(b1)   As provided in the contract between the Office of Administrative Hearings and the Equal Employment Opportunity Commission, a deferred charge for purposes of 42 U.S.C. § 2000e-5(c) or (d) is a charge that is filed by a State or local government employee covered under Chapter 126 of the General Statutes and alleges an unlawful employment practice prohibited under that Chapter or any other State law. A deferred charge may be filed with either agency.

The date a deferred charge is filed with either agency is considered to be a commencement of proceedings under State law for purposes of 42 U.S.C. § 2000e-5(c) or (d). The filing of a deferred charge automatically tolls the time limit under G.S. 126-7.2, 126-35, 126-38, and 150B-23(f) and any other State law that sets a time limit for filing a contested case under Article 3 of Chapter 150B of the General Statutes alleging an unlawful employment practice. These time limits are tolled until the completion of the investigation and of any informal methods of resolution pursued pursuant to subsection (d) of this section.

(c)   In investigating charges an employee of the Civil Rights Division of the Office of Administrative Hearings specifically designated by an order of the Chief Administrative Law Judge filed in the pending case may administer oaths and affirmations.

(c1)   In investigating charges, an employee of the Civil Rights Division shall have access at reasonable times to State premises, records, and documents relevant to the charge and shall have the right to examine, photograph, and copy evidence. Any challenge to the Civil Rights Division to investigate the deferred charge shall not constitute grounds for denial or refusal to produce or allow access to the investigative evidence.

(d)   Any charge not resolved by informal methods of conference, conciliation or persuasion may be heard as a contested case as provided in Article 3 of Chapter 150B of the General Statutes.

(e)   An order entered by an administrative law judge after a contested case hearing on the merits of a deferred charge is a final agency decision and is binding on the parties. The administrative law judge may order whatever remedial action is appropriate to give full relief consistent with the requirements of federal statutes or regulations or State statutes or rules.

(f)   In addition to the authority vested in G.S. 7A-756 and G.S. 150B-33, an administrative law judge may monitor compliance with any negotiated settlement, conciliation agreement or order entered in a deferred case.

(g)   The standards of confidentiality established by federal statute or regulation for discrimination charges shall apply to deferred cases investigated or heard by the Office of Administrative Hearings.

(h)   Nothing in this section shall be construed as limiting the authority or right of any federal agency to act under any federal statute or regulation.

(i)   This section shall be broadly construed to further the general purposes stated in this section and the specific purposes of the particular provisions involved. (1987 (Reg. Sess., 1988), c. 1111, s. 14(c); 1993, c. 234, s. 1; 1997-513, s. 1; 1998-212, s. 22; 2011-398, s. 28.)

§ 7A-760. Number and status of employees; staff assignments; role of State Personnel Commission.

(a)   The number of administrative law judges and employees of the Office of Administrative Hearings shall be established by the General Assembly. The Chief Administrative Law Judge is exempt from provisions of the North Carolina Human Resources Act as provided by G.S. 126-5(c1)(26). All other employees of the Office of Administrative Hearings are subject to the North Carolina Human Resources Act.

(b)   The Chief Administrative Law Judge shall designate, from among the employees of the Office of Administrative Hearings, the Director and staff of the Rules Review Commission. (2006-66, s. 18.2(d); 2006-221, s. 20; 2013-382, s. 9.1(c).)

§ 7A-761. Reserved for future codification purposes.

§ 7A-762. Reserved for future codification purposes.

§ 7A-763. Reserved for future codification purposes.

§ 7A-764. Reserved for future codification purposes.

§ 7A-765. Reserved for future codification purposes.

§ 7A-766. Reserved for future codification purposes.

§ 7A-767. Reserved for future codification purposes.

§ 7A-768. Reserved for future codification purposes.

§ 7A-769. Reserved for future codification purposes.

Vision Books Order Form

Fax Orders:	1-980-299-5965
Phone Orders:	1-704-898-0770
E-mail Orders:	www.visionbooks.org
Mail Orders:	Vision Books, LLC
	P.O. Box 42406
	Charlotte, NC 28215

Shipp To:
Name_____
Address_____
City_____State_____Zip_____
Phone_____Fax_____
Email_____@_____

Bill To: We can bill a third party on your behalf.
Name_____
Address_____
City_____State_____Zip_____
Phone____(   )_____Fax_____
Email_____@_____

Pamphlet Number ($15.00 Each)	Qty	Total Cost
_____	_____	_____
_____	_____	_____
_____	_____	_____
_____	_____	_____
_____	_____	_____
_____	_____	_____
_____	_____	_____
_____	_____	_____
Full Volume Set 1-92	92 Pamphlets	1,380.00

Free Shipping Shipping & Handling on Full Volume Orders
Add $1.00 Shipping & Handling per pamphlet $_____

Total Cost $_____

Thank You for Your Support. Management!

DID YOU ENJOY THIS BOOK?

Vision Books, LLC would like to hear from you! If you or someone you know has been fasely imprisoned, we would like to hear your story. If the 'North Carolina Criminal Law and Procedure' has had an effect in your life or if you have suggestions, we would like to hear from you. Send your letters to:

Vision Books, LLC
Attn: Staff Writers
P.O. Box 42406
Charlotte, NC 28215
Email: staff@visionbooks.org

Order Additional Copies:

Fax Orders: 1-980-299-5965

Phone Orders: 1-704-898-0770

E-mail Orders: www.visionbooks.org

Mail Orders: Vision Books, LLC
                         P.O. Box 42406
                         Charlotte, NC 28215

www.ingramcontent.com/pod-product-compliance
Lightning Source LLC
Chambersburg PA
CBHW051515170526
45165CB00002B/476